GOD'S PROMISES®
for
every day

THOMAS NELSON
Since 1798

NASHVILLE DALLAS MEXICO CITY RIO DE JANEIRO BEIJING

ISBN 978-0-8499-6268-4

Printed in the United States of America

Presented to

_____

_____

by

_____

_____

on

_____

_____

CONTENTS

WHAT THE BIBLE HAS TO SAY ABOUT

TRUTH FROM THE BIBLE ABOUT

WHAT YOU CAN DO TO

GOD'S PLAN OF SALVATION

Jesus Is Your . . .

Savior

He saved us because of his mercy. It was not because of good deeds we did to be right with him. He saved us through the washing that made us new people through the Holy Spirit. God poured out richly upon us that Holy Spirit through Jesus Christ our Savior.

Titus 3:5–6

We have seen and can testify that the Father sent his Son to be the Savior of the world.

1 John 4:14

My soul praises the Lord; my heart rejoices in God my Savior.

Luke 1:46b–47

The Son of Man came to find lost people and save them.

Luke 19:10

God loved the world so much that he gave his one and only Son so that whoever believes in him may not be lost, but have eternal life.

John 3:16

God makes people right with himself through their faith in Jesus Christ. This is true for all who believe in Christ, because all people are the same: All have sinned and are not good enough for God's glory, and all need to be made right with God by his grace, which is a free gift. They need to be made free from sin through Jesus Christ.

Romans 3:22–24

But God's mercy is great, and he loved us very much. Though we were spiritually dead because of the things we did against God, he gave us new life with Christ. You have been saved by God's grace.

Ephesians 2:4–5

I tell you the truth, whoever believes has eternal life.

John 6:47

I mean that you have been saved by grace through believing. You did not save yourselves; it was a gift from God. It was not the result of your own efforts, so you cannot brag about it.

Ephesians 2:8–9

If you use your mouth to say, "Jesus is Lord," and if you believe in your heart that God raised Jesus from the dead, you will be saved.

Romans 10:9

If anyone belongs to Christ, there is a new creation. The old things have gone; everything is made new!

2 Corinthians 5:17

But suffer with me for the Good News. God, who gives us the strength to do that, saved us and made us his holy people. That was not because of anything we did ourselves but because of God's purpose and grace. That grace was given to us through Christ Jesus before time began.

2 Timothy 1:8b–9

But the Lord saved them for his own sake, to show his great power.

Psalm 106:8

Lord

So God raised him to the highest place. God made his name greater than every other name so that every knee will bow to the name of Jesus— everyone in heaven, on earth, and under the earth. And everyone will confess that Jesus Christ is Lord and bring glory to God the Father.

Philippians 2:9–11

If you use your mouth to say, "Jesus is Lord," and if you believe in your heart that God raised Jesus from the dead, you will be saved. We believe with our hearts, and so we are made right with God. And we use our mouths to say that we believe, and so we are saved.

Romans 10:9–10

Why do you call me, "Lord, Lord," but do not do what I say?

Luke 6:46

Do not offer the parts of your body to serve sin, as things to be used in doing evil. Instead, offer yourselves to God as people who have died and now live. Offer the parts of your body to God to be used in doing good. Sin will not be your master, because you are not under law but under God's grace. So what should we do? Should we sin because we are under grace and not under law? No! Surely you know that when you give yourselves like slaves to obey someone, then you are really slaves of that person. The person you obey is your master. You can follow sin, which brings spiritual death, or you can obey God, which makes you right with him.

Romans 6:13–16

So brothers and sisters, since God has shown us great mercy, I beg you to offer your lives as a living sacrifice to him. Your offering must be only for God and pleasing to him, which is the spiritual way for you to worship. Do not change yourselves to be like the people of this world, but be changed within by a new way of thinking. Then you will be able to decide what God wants for you; you will know what is good and pleasing to him and what is perfect.

Romans 12:1–2

You should know that your body is a temple for the Holy Spirit who is in you. You have received the Holy Spirit from God. So you do not belong to yourselves, because you were bought by God for a price. So honor God with your bodies.

1 Corinthians 6:19–20

So, all the people of Israel should know this truly: God has made Jesus—the man you nailed to the cross—both Lord and Christ.

Acts 2:36

If we live, we are living for the Lord, and if we die, we are dying for the Lord. So living or dying, we belong to the Lord.

Romans 14:8

Praise the Lord, God our Savior, who helps us every day.

Psalm 68:19

But I am close to God, and that is good. The Lord GOD is my protection. I will tell all that you have done.

Psalm 73.28

Lord, you are kind and forgiving and have great love for those who call to you.

Psalm 86:5

The Lord GOD helps me, so I will not be ashamed. I will be determined, and I know I will not be disgraced.

Isaiah 50:7

Love the Lord your God with all your heart, all your soul, all your mind, and all your strength.

Mark 12:30

For David said this about him: "I keep the Lord before me always. Because he is close by my side, I will not be hurt."

Acts 2:25

Love

But God shows his great love for us in this way: Christ died for us while we were still sinners.

Romans 5:8

God loved the world so much that he gave his one and only Son so that whoever believes in him may not be lost, but have eternal life.

John 3:16

Dear friends, we should love each other, because love comes from God. Everyone who loves has become God's child and knows God. Whoever does not love does not know God, because God is love. This is how God showed his love to us: He sent his one and only Son into the world so that we could have life through him. This is what real love is: It is not our love for God; it is God's love for us in sending his Son to be the way to take away our sins. Dear friends, if God loved us that much we also should love each other. No one has ever seen God, but if we love each other, God lives in us, and his love is made perfect in us.

1 John 4:7–12

And so we know the love that God has for us, and we trust that love. God is love. Those who live in love live in God, and God lives in them. We love because God first loved us.

1 John 4:16, 19

I loved you as the Father loved me. Now remain in my love. I have obeyed my Father's commands, and I remain in his love. In the same way, if you obey my commands, you will remain in my love. I have told you these things so that you can have the same joy I have and so that your joy will be the fullest possible joy. This is my command: Love each other as I have loved you. The greatest love a person can show is to die for his friends. This is my command: Love each other.

John 15:9–13, 17

I pray that Christ will live in your hearts by faith and that your life will be strong in love and be built on love. And I pray that you and all God's holy people will have the power to understand the greatness of Christ's love—how wide and how long and how high and how deep that love is. Christ's love is greater than anyone can ever know, but I pray that you will be able to know that love. Then you can be filled with the fullness of God.

Ephesians 3:17–19

I love those who love me, and those who seek me find me.

Proverbs 8:17

And from far away the LORD appeared to his people and said, "I love you people with a love that will last forever. That is why I have continued showing you kindness."

Jeremiah 31:3

And I will make you my promised bride forever.
I will be good and fair; I will show you my love and
mercy.

Hosea 2:19

Those who know my commands and obey them are the
ones who love me, and my Father will love those who love
me. I will love them and will show myself to them.

John 14:21

The LORD shows his true love every day. At night
I have a song, and I pray to my living God.

Psalm 42:8

So these three things continue forever: faith, hope,
and love. And the greatest of these is love.

1 Corinthians 13:13

Yes, I am sure that neither death, nor life, nor angels, nor ruling spirits, nothing now, nothing in the
future, no powers, nothing above us, nothing below
us, nor anything else in the whole world will ever be
able to separate us from the love of God that is in
Christ Jesus our Lord.

Romans 8:38–39

Peace

You, LORD, give true peace to those who depend on you, because they trust you.

Isaiah 26:3

But now in Christ Jesus, you who were far away from God are brought near through the blood of Christ's death. Christ himself is our peace. He made both Jewish people and those who are not Jews one people. They were separated as if there were a wall between them, but Christ broke down that wall of hate by giving his own body.

Ephesians 2:13–14

A child has been born to us; God has given a son to us. He will be responsible for leading the people. His name will be Wonderful Counselor, Powerful God, Father Who Lives Forever, Prince of Peace. Power and peace will be in his kingdom and will continue to grow forever. He will rule as king on David's throne and over David's kingdom. He will make it strong by ruling with justice and goodness from now on and forever. The LORD All-Powerful will do this because of his strong love for his people.

Isaiah 9:6–7

The God who brings peace will soon defeat Satan and give you power over him. The grace of our Lord Jesus be with you.

Romans 16:20

LORD, all our success is because of what you have done, so give us peace.

Isaiah 26:12

Do what you learned and received from me, what I told you, and what you saw me do. And the God who gives peace will be with you.

Philippians 4:9

Since we have been made right with God by our faith, we have peace with God. This happened through our Lord Jesus Christ.

Romans 5:1

Let the peace that Christ gives control your thinking, because you were all called together in one body to have peace. Always be thankful.

Colossians 3:15

I go to bed and sleep in peace, because, LORD, only you keep me safe.

Psalm 4:8

The LORD gives strength to his people; the LORD blesses his people with peace.

Psalm 29:11

I leave you peace; my peace I give you. I do not give it to you as the world does. So don't let your hearts be troubled or afraid.

John 14:27

Do not worry about anything, but pray and ask God for everything you need, always giving thanks. And God's peace, which is so great we cannot understand it, will keep your hearts and minds in Christ Jesus.

Philippians 4:6–7

Forgiveness

Because of his love, God had already decided to make us his own children through Jesus Christ. That was what he wanted and what pleased him, and it brings praise to God because of his wonderful grace. God gave that grace to us freely, in Christ, the One he loves. In Christ we are set free by the blood of his death, and so we have forgiveness of sins. How rich is God's grace.

Ephesians 1:5–7

You forgave the guilt of the people and covered all their sins.

Psalm 85:2

If anyone belongs to Christ, there is a new creation. The old things have gone; everything is made new!

2 Corinthians 5:17

He has taken our sins away from us as far as the east is from west.

Psalm 103:12

My dear children, I write this letter to you so you will not sin. But if anyone does sin, we have a helper in the presence of the Father— Jesus Christ, the one who does what is right.

1 John 2:1

But if we confess our sins, he will forgive our sins,

because we can trust God to do what is right. He will cleanse us from all the wrongs we have done.

1 John 1:9

I, I am the One who forgives all your sins, for my sake; I will not remember your sins.

Isaiah 43:25

I will forgive them for the wicked things they did, and I will not remember their sins anymore.

Hebrews 8:12

The wicked should stop doing wrong, and they should stop their evil thoughts. They should return to the LORD so he may have mercy on them. They should come to our God, because he will freely forgive them.

Isaiah 55:7

Get along with each other, and forgive each other. If someone does wrong to you, forgive that person because the Lord forgave you.

Colossians 3:13

When you are praying, if you are angry with someone, forgive him so that your Father in heaven will also forgive your sins.

Mark 11:25

When you were spiritually dead because of your sins and because you were not free from the power of your sinful self, God made you alive with Christ, and he forgave all our sins.

Colossians 2:13

They sinned against me, but I will wash away that sin. They did evil and turned away from me, but I will forgive them.

Jeremiah 33:8

The Lord says, "Come, let us talk about these things. Though your sins are like scarlet, they can be as white as snow. Though your sins are deep red, they can be white like wool."

Isaiah 1:18

Happy is the person whose sins are forgiven, whose wrongs are pardoned. Happy is the person whom the Lord does not consider guilty and in whom there is nothing false.

Psalm 32:1–2

Righteousness

Christ had no sin, but God made him become sin so that in Christ we could become right with God.

2 Corinthians 5:21

Because of God you are in Christ Jesus, who has become for us wisdom from God. In Christ we are put right with God, and have been made holy, and have been set free from sin.

1 Corinthians 1:30

I think that all things are worth nothing compared with the greatness of knowing Christ Jesus my Lord. Because of him, I have lost all those things, and now I know they are worthless trash. This allows me to have Christ and to belong to him. Now I am right with God, not because I followed the law, but because I believed in Christ. God uses my faith to make me right with him.

Philippians 3:8–9

The Scriptures say the same thing about Abraham: "Abraham believed God, and God accepted Abraham's faith, and that faith made him right with God." So you should know that the true children of Abraham are those who have faith.

Galatians 3:6–7

God makes people right with himself through their

faith in Jesus Christ. This is true for all who believe in Christ, because all people are the same.

Romans 3:22

All have sinned and are not good enough for God's glory, and all need to be made right with God by his grace, which is a free gift. They need to be made free from sin through Jesus Christ. God gave him as a way to forgive sin through faith in the blood of Jesus' death. This showed that God always does what is right and fair, as in the past when he was patient and did not punish people for their sins. And God gave Jesus to show today that he does what is right. God did this so he could judge rightly and so he could make right any person who has faith in Jesus.

Romans 3:23–26

But people cannot do any work that will make them right with God. So they must trust in him, who makes even evil people right in his sight. Then God accepts their faith, and that makes them right with him.

Romans 4:5

One man sinned, and so death ruled all people because of that one man. But now those people who accept God's full grace and the great gift of being made right with him will surely have true life and rule through the one man, Jesus Christ.

Romans 5:17

But when the kindness and love of God our Savior was shown, he saved us because of his mercy. It was not because of good deeds we did to be right with him. He saved us through the washing that made us new people through the Holy Spirit.

Titus 3:4–5

The law was without power, because the law was made weak by our sinful selves. But God did what the law could not do. He sent his own Son to earth with the same human life that others use for sin. By sending his Son to be an offering to pay for sin, God used a human life to destroy sin. He did this so that we could be the kind of people the law correctly wants us to be. Now we do not live following our sinful selves, but we live following the Spirit.

Romans 8:3–4

So what does all this mean? Those who are not Jews were not trying to make themselves right with God, but they were made right with God because of their faith.

Romans 9:30

Your body will always be dead because of sin. But if Christ is in you, then the Spirit gives you life, because Christ made you right with God.

Romans 8:10

God knew them before he made the world, and he decided that they would be like his Son so that Jesus would be the firstborn of many brothers. God planned for them to be like his Son; and those he planned to be like his Son, he also called; and those he called, he also made right with him; and those he made right, he also glorified.

Romans 8:29–30

"I will build you using fairness. You will be safe from those who would hurt you, so you will have nothing to fear. Nothing will come to make you afraid. I will not send anyone to attack you, and you will defeat those who do attack you. See, I made the blacksmith. He fans the fire to make it hotter, and he makes the kind of tool he wants. In the same way I have made the destroyer to destroy. So no weapon that is used against you will defeat you. You will show that those who speak against you are wrong. These are the good things my servants receive. Their victory comes from me," says the Lord.

Isaiah 54:14–17

We believe with our hearts, and so we are made right with God. And we use our mouths to say that we believe, and so we are saved.

Romans 10:10

Deliverer

The Lord God has put his Spirit in me, because the Lord has appointed me to tell the good news to the poor. He has sent me to comfort those whose hearts are broken, to tell the captives they are free, and to tell the prisoners they are released.

Isaiah 61:1

Then you will know the truth, and the truth will make you free. So if the Son makes you free, you will be truly free.

John 8:32, 36

Through Christ Jesus the law of the Spirit that brings life made me free from the law that brings sin and death.

Romans 8:2

The Lord is the Spirit, and where the Spirit of the Lord is, there is freedom.

2 Corinthians 3:17

But now you are free from sin and have become slaves of God. This brings you a life that is only for God, and this gives you life forever.

Romans 6:22

God, you have caused the nation to grow and made the people happy. And they have shown their happiness to you, like the joy during harvest time, like the joy of people taking what they have won in war. Like the time you defeated Midian, you have taken away their heavy load and the heavy pole from their backs and the rod the enemy used to punish them.

Isaiah 9:3–4

The Lord has put his Spirit in me, because he appointed me to tell the Good News to the poor. He has sent me to tell the captives they are free and to tell the blind that they can see again. God sent me to free those who have been treated unfairly and to announce the time when the Lord will show his kindness.

Luke 4:18–19

Listen, I have given you power to walk on snakes and scorpions, power that is greater than the enemy has. So nothing will hurt you.

Luke 10:19

And those who believe will be able to do these things as proof: They will use my name to force out demons. They will speak in new languages.

Mark 16:17

And our brothers and sisters defeated him by the blood of the Lamb's death and by the message they preached. They did not love their lives so much that they were afraid of death.

Revelation 12:11

My dear friends, many false prophets have gone out into the world. So do not believe every spirit, but test the spirits to see if they are from God. This is how you can know God's Spirit: Every spirit who confesses that Jesus Christ came to earth as a human is from God. And every spirit who refuses to say this about Jesus is not from God. It is the spirit of the enemy of Christ, which you have heard is coming, and now he is already in the world. My dear children, you belong to God and have defeated them; because God's Spirit, who is in you, is greater than the devil, who is in the world.

1 John 4:1–4

Fellowship

We announce to you what we have seen and heard, because we want you also to have fellowship with us. Our fellowship is with God the Father and with his Son, Jesus Christ.

1 John 1:3

God, who has called you to share everything with his Son, Jesus Christ our Lord, is faithful.

1 Corinthians 1:9

Here I am! I stand at the door and knock. If you hear my voice and open the door, I will come in and eat with you, and you will eat with me.

Revelation 3:20

Jesus answered, "If people love me, they will obey my teaching. My Father will love them, and we will come to them and make our home with them."

John 14:23

"Shout and be glad, Jerusalem. I am coming, and I will live among you," says the Lord.

Zechariah 2:10

This is true because if two or three people come together in my name, I am there with them.

Matthew 18:20

Those who know my commands and obey them are the ones who love me, and my Father will love those who love me. I will love them and will show myself to them.

John 14:21

Remain in me, and I will remain in you. A branch cannot produce fruit alone but must remain in the vine. In the same way, you cannot produce fruit alone but must remain in me. I am the vine, and you are the branches. If any remain in me and I remain in them, they produce much fruit. But without me they can do nothing. If you remain in me and follow my teachings, you can ask anything you want, and it will be given to you.

John 15:4–5, 7

Does your life in Christ give you strength? Does his love comfort you? Do we share together in the spirit? Do you have mercy and kindness? If so, make me very happy by having the same thoughts, sharing the same love, and having one mind and purpose.

Philippians 2:1–2

I am a friend to everyone who fears you, to anyone who obeys your orders.

Psalm 119:63

Live a life of love just as Christ loved us and gave himself for us as a sweet-smelling offering and sacrifice to God. Speak to each other with psalms, hymns, and spiritual songs, singing and making music in your hearts to the Lord. Because we are parts of his body.

Ephesians 5:2, 19, 30

Here is the message we have heard from Christ and now announce to you: God is light, and in him there is no darkness at all. So if we say we have fellowship with God, but we continue living in darkness, we are liars and do not follow the truth. But if we live in the light, as God is in the light, we can share fellowship with each other. Then the blood of Jesus, God's Son, cleanses us from every sin.

1 John 1:5–7

Example

This is what you were called to do, because Christ suffered for you and gave you an example to follow. So you should do as he did.

1 Peter 2:21

Whoever says that he lives in God must live as Jesus lived.

1 John 2:6

You are God's children whom he loves, so try to be like him. Live a life of love just as Christ loved us and gave himself for us as a sweet-smelling offering and sacrifice to God.

Ephesians 5:1–2

In your lives you must think and act like Christ Jesus. Christ himself was like God in everything. But he did not think that being equal with God was something to be used for his own benefit. But he gave up his place with God and made himself nothing. He was born to be a man and became like a servant. And when he was living as a man, he humbled himself and was fully obedient to God, even when that caused his death—death on a cross.

Philippians 2:5–8

But it should not be that way among you. Whoever wants to become great among you must serve the rest of you like a servant. Whoever wants to become the first among you must serve all of you like a slave. In the same way, the Son of Man did not come to be served. He came to serve others and to give his life as a ransom for many people.

Mark 10:43–45

If I, your Lord and Teacher, have washed your feet, you also should wash each other's feet. I did this as an example so that you should do as I have done for you.

John 13:14–15

I give you a new command: Love each other. You must love each other as I have loved you.

John 13:34

This is how we know what real love is: Jesus gave his life for us. So we should give our lives for our brothers and sisters.

1 John 3:16

Patience and encouragement come from God. And I pray that God will help you all agree with each other the way Christ Jesus wants. Then you will all be joined together, and you will give glory to God the Father of our Lord Jesus Christ. Christ accepted you, so you should accept each other, which will bring glory to God.

Romans 15:5–7

Get along with each other, and forgive each other. If someone does wrong to you, forgive that person because the Lord forgave you.

Colossians 3:13

Let us look only to Jesus, the One who began our faith and who makes it perfect. He suffered death on the cross. But he accepted the shame as if it were nothing because of the joy that God put before him. And now he is sitting at the right side of God's throne. Think about Jesus' example. He held on while wicked people were doing evil things to him. So do not get tired and stop trying.

Hebrews 12:2–3

Friend

I am a friend to everyone who fears you, to anyone who obeys your orders.

Psalm 119:63

Some friends may ruin you, but a real friend will be more loyal than a brother.

Proverbs 18:24

Keep your lives free from the love of money, and be satisfied with what you have. God has said, "I will never leave you; I will never forget you."

Hebrews 13:5

I no longer call you servants, because a servant does not know what his master is doing. But I call you friends, because I have made known to you everything I heard from my Father. You did not choose me; I chose you. And I gave you this work: to go and produce fruit, fruit that will last. Then the Father will give you anything you ask for in my name.

John 15:15–16

But if we live in the light, as God is in the light, we can share fellowship with each other. Then the blood of Jesus, God's Son, cleanses us from every sin.

1 John 1:7

"The mountains may disappear, and the hills may

come to an end, but my love will never disappear; my promise of peace will not come to an end," says the LORD who shows mercy to you.

Isaiah 54:10

Here I am! I stand at the door and knock. If you hear my voice and open the door, I will come in and eat with you, and you will eat with me.

Revelation 3:20

Come near to God, and God will come near to you. You sinners, clean sin out of your lives. You who are trying to follow God and the world at the same time, make your thinking pure.

James 4:8

If my father and mother leave me, the LORD will take me in.

Psalm 27:10

This is my command: Love each other as I have loved you. The greatest love a person can show is to die for his friends. You are my friends if you do what I command you.

John 15:12–14

God, who has called you to share everything with his Son, Jesus Christ our Lord, is faithful.

1 Corinthians 1:9

We announce to you what we have seen and heard, because we want you also to have fellowship with us.

Our fellowship is with God the Father and with his Son, Jesus Christ.

1 John 1:3

I will not leave you all alone like orphans; I will come back to you.

John 14:18

Brother

My true brother and sister and mother are those who do what my Father in heaven wants.

Matthew 12:50

Jesus, who makes people holy, and those who are made holy are from the same family. So he is not ashamed to call them his brothers and sisters.

Hebrews 2:11

God knew them before he made the world, and he decided that they would be like his Son so that Jesus would be the firstborn of many brothers.

Romans 8:29

You were all baptized into Christ, and so you were all clothed with Christ. This means that you are all children of God through faith in Christ Jesus.

Galatians 3:26–27

But to all who did accept him and believe in him he gave the right to become children of God.

John 1:12

Now you who are not Jewish are not foreigners or strangers any longer, but are citizens together with God's holy people. You belong to God's family.

Ephesians 2:19

The Father has loved us so much that we are called

children of God. And we really are his children. The reason the people in the world do not know us is that they have not known him.

1 John 3:1

Since you are God's children, God sent the Spirit of his Son into your hearts, and the Spirit cries out, "Father." So now you are not a slave; you are God's child, and God will give you the blessing he promised, because you are his child.

Galatians 4:6–7

The true children of God are those who let God's Spirit lead them.

Romans 8:14

Dear friends, now we are children of God, and we have not yet been shown what we will be in the future. But we know that when Christ comes again, we will be like him, because we will see him as he really is.

1 John 3:2

Protector

When you pass through the waters, I will be with you. When you cross rivers, you will not drown. When you walk through fire, you will not be burned, nor will the flames hurt you.

Isaiah 43:2

But, LORD, you are my shield, my wonderful God who gives me courage.

Psalm 3:3

The Lord searches all the earth for people who have given themselves completely to him.

2 Chronicles 16:9a

The LORD your God will go ahead of you and fight for you as he did in Egypt; you saw him do it.

Deuteronomy 1:30

But the Lord is faithful and will give you strength and will protect you from the Evil One.

2 Thessalonians 3:3

If you listen carefully to all he says and do everything that I tell you, I will be an enemy to your enemies. I will fight all who fight against you.

Exodus 23:22

He protects those who are loyal to him, but evil people will be silenced in darkness. Power is not the key to success.

1 Samuel 2:9

You have been my protection, like a strong tower against my enemies.

Psalm 61:3

The LORD your God is with you; the mighty One will save you. He will rejoice over you. You will rest in his love; he will sing and be joyful about you.

Zephaniah 3:17

The Lord sees the good people and listens to their prayers. But the Lord is against those who do evil. If you are trying hard to do good, no one can really hurt you.

1 Peter 3:12–13

The everlasting God is your place of safety, and his arms will hold you up forever. He will force your enemy out ahead of you, saying, "Destroy the enemy!"

Deuteronomy 33:27

At your side one thousand people may die, or even ten thousand right beside you, but you will not be hurt.

Psalm 91:7

Then people from the west will fear the Lord, and people from the east will fear his glory. The Lord will come quickly like a fast-flowing river, driven by the breath of the Lord.

Isaiah 59:19

Security

Praise be to the God and Father of our Lord Jesus Christ. In God's great mercy he has caused us to be born again into a living hope, because Jesus Christ rose from the dead. Now we hope for the blessings God has for his children. These blessings, which cannot be destroyed or be spoiled or lose their beauty, are kept in heaven for you. God's power protects you through your faith until salvation is shown to you at the end of time.

1 Peter 1:3–5

My sheep listen to my voice; I know them, and they follow me. I give them eternal life, and they will never die, and no one can steal them out of my hand. My Father gave my sheep to me. He is greater than all, and no person can steal my sheep out of my Father's hand. The Father and I are one.

John 10:27–30

Can anything separate us from the love Christ has for us? Can troubles or problems or sufferings or hunger or nakedness or danger or violent death? Yes, I am sure that neither death, nor life, nor angels, nor ruling spirits, nothing now, nothing in the future, no powers, nothing above us, nothing below us, nor anything else in the whole world will ever be able to separate us from the love of God that is in Christ Jesus our Lord.

Romans 8:35, 38–39

God began doing a good work in you, and I am sure he will continue it until it is finished when Jesus Christ comes again.

Philippians 1:6

But the Lord is faithful and will give you strength and will protect you from the Evil One.

2 Thessalonians 3:3

The Father gives me my people. Every one of them will come to me, and I will always accept them.

John 6:37

God is strong and can help you not to fall. He can bring you before his glory without any wrong in you and can give you great joy. He is the only God, the One who saves us. To him be glory, greatness, power, and authority through Jesus Christ our Lord for all time past, now, and forever. Amen.

Jude 24–25

Look up to the skies. Who created all these stars? He leads out the army of heaven one by one and calls all the stars by name. Because he is strong and powerful, not one of them is missing.

Isaiah 40:26

Surely your goodness and love will be with me all my life, and I will live in the house of the Lord forever.

Psalm 23:6

Don't work for the food that spoils. Work for the food that stays good always and gives eternal life. The Son of Man will give you this food, because on him God the Father has put his power.

John 6:27

He put his mark on us to show that we are his, and he put his Spirit in our hearts to be a guarantee for all he has promised.

2 Corinthians 1:22

So it is with you. When you heard the true teaching the Good News about your salvation you believed in Christ. And in Christ, God put his special mark of ownership on you by giving you the Holy Spirit that he had promised. That Holy Spirit is the guarantee that we will receive what God promised for his people until God gives full freedom to those who are his to bring praise to God's glory.

Ephesians 1:13–14

And do not make the Holy Spirit sad. The Spirit is God's proof that you belong to him. God gave you the Spirit to show that God will make you free when the final day comes.

Ephesians 4:30

We want each of you to go on with the same hard work all your lives so you will surely get what you hope for. We do not want you to become lazy. Be like those who through faith and patience will receive what God has promised. These two things cannot change: God cannot lie when he makes a promise, and he cannot lie when he makes an oath. These things encourage us who came to God for safety. They give us strength to hold on to the hope we have been given. We have this hope as an anchor for the soul, sure and strong. It enters behind the curtain in the Most Holy Place in heaven, where Jesus has gone ahead of us and for us. He has become the high priest forever, a priest like Melchizedek.

Hebrews 6:11–12, 18–20

Answer

And God can give you more blessings than you need. Then you will always have plenty of everything —enough to give to every good work.

2 Corinthians 9:8

My God will use his wonderful riches in Christ Jesus to give you everything you need.

Philippians 4:19

So I tell you to believe that you have received the things you ask for in prayer, and God will give them to you.

Mark 11:24

We are not saying that we can do this work ourselves. It is God who makes us able to do all that we do.

2 Corinthians 3:5

I know how to live when I am poor, and I know how to live when I have plenty. I have learned the secret of being happy at any time in everything that happens, when I have enough to eat and when I go hungry, when I have more than I need and when I do not have enough. I can do all things through Christ, because he gives me strength.

Philippians 4:12–13

And you will know that God's power is very great for us who believe. That power is the same as the great strength God used to raise Christ from the dead and put him at his right side in the heavenly world.

Ephesians 1:19–20

But he said to me, "My grace is enough for you. When you are weak, my power is made perfect in you." So I am very happy to brag about my weaknesses. Then Christ's power can live in me.

2 Corinthians 12:9

But in all these things we have full victory through God who showed his love for us.

Romans 8:37

Praise be to the God and Father of our Lord Jesus Christ. In Christ, God has given us every spiritual blessing in the heavenly world.

Ephesians 1:3

If you remain in me and follow my teachings, you can ask anything you want, and it will be given to you.

John 15:7

And if you ask for anything in my name, I will do it for you so that the Father's glory will be shown through the Son.

John 14:13

In that day you will not ask me for anything. I tell you the truth, my Father will give you anything you ask for in my name. Until now you have not asked for anything in my name. Ask and you will receive, so that your joy will be the fullest possible joy.

John 16:23–24

If you believe, you will get anything you ask for in prayer.

Matthew 21:22

So what should we say about this? If God is with us, no one can defeat us. He did not spare his own Son but gave him for us all. So with Jesus, God will surely give us all things.

Romans 8:31–32

Jesus has the power of God, by which he has given us everything we need to live and to serve God. We have these things because we know him. Jesus called us by his glory and goodness. Through these he gave us the very great and precious promises. With these gifts you can share in being like God, and the world will not ruin you with its evil desires.

2 Peter 1:3–4

My whole being, praise the LORD and do not forget all his kindnesses. He forgives all my sins and heals all my diseases. He saves my life from the grave and loads me with love and mercy.

Psalm 103:2–4

Satisfaction

Those who want to do right more than anything else are happy, because God will fully satisfy them.

Matthew 5:6

Enjoy serving the LORD, and he will give you what you want. Depend on the LORD; trust him, and he will take care of you.

Psalm 37:4–5

They were hungry and thirsty, and they were discouraged. He satisfies the thirsty and fills up the hungry.

Psalm 107:5, 9

He satisfies me with good things and makes me young again, like the eagle.

Psalm 103:5

Then you will have plenty to eat and be full. You will praise the name of the LORD your God, who has done miracles for you. My people will never again be shamed.

Joel 2:26

Then Jesus said, "I am the bread that gives life. Whoever comes to me will never be hungry, and whoever believes in me will never be thirsty."

John 6:35

Poor people will eat until they are full; those who

look to the LORD will praise him. May your hearts live forever!

Psalm 22:26

Jesus answered, "Everyone who drinks this water will be thirsty again, but whoever drinks the water I give will never be thirsty. The water I give will become a spring of water gushing up inside that person, giving eternal life."

John 4:13–14

Then the LORD became concerned about his land and felt sorry for his people. He said to them: "I will send you grain, new wine, and olive oil, so that you will have plenty. No more will I shame you among the nations."

Joel 2:18-19

If you feed those who are hungry and take care of the needs of those who are troubled, then your light will shine in the darkness, and you will be bright like sunshine at noon. The Lord will always lead you. He will satisfy your needs in dry lands and give strength to your bones. You will be like a garden that has much water, like a spring that never runs dry.

Isaiah 58:10-11

All living things look to you for food, and you give it to them at the right time. You open your hand, and you satisfy all living things. Everything the Lord does is right. He is loyal to all he has made.

Psalm 145:15–17

Why spend your money on something that is not real food? Why work for something that doesn't really satisfy you? Listen closely to me, and you will eat what is good; your soul will enjoy the rich food that satisfies.

Isaiah 55:2

"The priests will have more than enough sacrifices, and my people will be filled with the good things I give them!" says the LORD.

Jeremiah 31:14

I will be content as if I had eaten the best foods. My lips will sing, and my mouth will praise you. I remember you while I'm lying in bed; I think about you through the night. I stay close to you; you support me with your right hand.

Psalm 63:5–6, 8

He did not spare his own Son but gave him for us all. So with Jesus, God will surely give us all things.

Romans 8:32

Everything

My God will use his wonderful riches in Christ Jesus to give you everything you need.

Philippians 4:19

I can do all things through Christ, because he gives me strength.

Philippians 4:13

But in all these things we have full victory through God who showed his love for us.

Romans 8:37

So you should not brag about human leaders. All things belong to you: Paul, Apollos, and Peter; the world, life, death, the present, and the future—all these belong to you. And you belong to Christ, and Christ belongs to God.

1 Corinthians 3:21–23

You are already clean because of the words I have spoken to you. If you remain in me and follow my teachings, you can ask anything you want, and it will be given to you.

John 15:3, 7

All that the Father has is mine. That is why I said that the Spirit will take what I have to say and tell it to you. In that day you will not ask me for anything. I tell you the truth, my Father will give you anything you ask for in my name.

John 16:15, 23

If you believe, you will get anything you ask for in prayer.

Matthew 21:22

So I tell you to believe that you have received the things you ask for in prayer, and God will give them to you.

Mark 11:24

Praise be to the God and Father of our Lord Jesus Christ. In Christ, God has given us every spiritual blessing in the heavenly world.

Ephesians 1:3

And God gives us what we ask for because we obey God's commands and do what pleases him. This is what God commands: that we believe in his Son, Jesus Christ, and that we love each other, just as he commanded.

1 John 3:22–23

Christ had no sin, but God made him become sin so that in Christ we could become right with God.

2 Corinthians 5:21

To me the only important thing about living is Christ, and dying would be profit for me.

Philippians 1:21

If anyone belongs to Christ, there is a new creation. The old things have gone; everything is made new!

2 Corinthians 5:17

With God's power working in us, God can do much, much more than anything we can ask or imagine. To him be glory in the church and in Christ Jesus for all time, forever and ever. Amen.

Ephesians 3:20–21

And God can give you more blessings than you need. Then you will always have plenty of everything—enough to give to every good work.

2 Corinthians 9:8

Praise the Lord, God our Savior, who helps us every day.

Psalm 68:19

What to Do When You Feel . . .

WHAT TO DO WHEN YOU FEEL

Discouraged

The people the LORD has freed will return and enter Jerusalem with joy. Their happiness will last forever. They will have joy and gladness, and all sadness and sorrow will be gone far away.

Isaiah 51:11

This makes you very happy, even though now for a short time different kinds of troubles may make you sad. These troubles come to prove that your faith is pure. This purity of faith is worth more than gold, which can be proved to be pure by fire but will ruin. But the purity of your faith will bring you praise and glory and honor when Jesus Christ is shown to you. You have not seen Christ, but still you love him. You cannot see him now, but you believe in him. So you are filled with a joy that cannot be explained, a joy full of glory. And you are receiving the goal of your faith the salvation of your souls.

1 Peter 1:6–9

Do not worry about anything, but pray and ask God for everything you need, always giving thanks. And God's peace, which is so great we cannot understand it, will keep your hearts and minds in Christ Jesus. Brothers and sisters, think about the things that are good and worthy of praise. Think about the things

that are true and honorable and right and pure and
beautiful and respected.

Philippians 4:6–8

LORD, even when I have trouble all around me,
you will keep me alive. When my enemies are angry,
you will reach down and save me by your power.

Psalm 138:7

Jesus said, "Don't let your hearts be troubled. Trust
in God, and trust in me."

John 14:1

I leave you peace; my peace I give you. I do not give
it to you as the world does. So don't let your hearts
be troubled or afraid.

John 14:27

We have troubles all around us, but we are not
defeated. We do not know what to do, but we do not
give up the hope of living. We are persecuted, but
God does not leave us. We are hurt sometimes, but
we are not destroyed.

2 Corinthians 4:8–9

So do not lose the courage you had in the past, which
has a great reward. You must hold on, so you can do
what God wants and receive what he has promised.

Hebrews 10:35–36

God began doing a good work in you, and I am

sure he will continue it until it is finished when Jesus Christ comes again.

Philippians 1:6

We must not become tired of doing good. We will receive our harvest of eternal life at the right time if we do not give up.

Galatians 6:9

All you who put your hope in the Lord be strong and brave.

Psalm 31:24

The Lord is my light and the one who saves me. I fear no one. The Lord protects my life; I am afraid of no one. Evil people may try to destroy my body. My enemies and those who hate me attack me, but they are overwhelmed and defeated. If an army surrounds me, I will not be afraid. If war breaks out, I will trust the Lord. I ask only one thing from the Lord. This is what I want: Let me live in the Lord's house all my life. Let me see the Lord's beauty and look with my own eyes at his Temple. During danger he will keep me safe in his shelter. He will hide me in his Holy Tent, or he will keep me safe on a high mountain. My head is higher than my enemies around me. I will offer joyful sacrifices in his Holy Tent. I will sing and praise the Lord. Lord, hear me when I call; have mercy and answer me. My heart said of you, "Go, worship him." So I come to worship you, Lord. Do not turn away from me. Do not turn your servant away in anger; you have helped me. Do not push me away or leave me alone, God, my Savior. If my father and mother leave me, the LORD will take me in. LORD, teach me your ways, and guide me to do what is right because I have enemies. Do not hand me over to my enemies, because they tell lies about me and say they will hurt me. I truly believe I will live to see the LORD's goodness. Wait for the LORD's help. Be strong and brave, and wait for the LORD's help.

Psalm 27:1–14

Worried

Give all your worries to him, because he cares about you.

1 Peter 5:7

Jesus said, "Don't let your hearts be troubled. Trust in God, and trust in me."

John 14:1

Do not worry about anything, but pray and ask God for everything you need, always giving thanks. And God's peace, which is so great we cannot understand it, will keep your hearts and minds in Christ Jesus.

Philippians 4:6–7

Let the peace that Christ gives control your thinking, because you were all called together in one body to have peace. Always be thankful.

Colossians 3:15

You, LORD, give true peace to those who depend on you, because they trust you.

Isaiah 26:3

My God will use his wonderful riches in Christ Jesus to give you everything you need.

Philippians 4:19

I go to bed and sleep in peace, because, LORD, only you keep me safe.

Psalm 4:8

So I tell you, don't worry about the food or drink you need to live, or about the clothes you need for your body. Life is more than food, and the body is more than clothes. Look at the birds in the air. They don't plant or harvest or store food in barns, but your heavenly Father feeds them. And you know that you are worth much more than the birds. You cannot add any time to your life by worrying about it. And why do you worry about clothes? Look at how the lilies in the field grow. They don't work or make clothes for themselves. But I tell you that even Solomon with his riches was not dressed as beautifully as one of these flowers. God clothes the grass in the field, which is alive today but tomorrow is thrown into the fire. So you can be even more sure that God will clothe you. Don't have so little faith! Don't worry and say, "What will we eat?" or "What will we drink?" or "What will we wear?" The people who don't know God keep trying to get these things, and your Father in heaven knows you need them. The thing you should want most is God's kingdom and doing what God wants. Then all these other things you need will be given to you. So don't worry about tomorrow, because tomorrow will have its own worries. Each day has enough trouble of its own.

Matthew 6:25–34

If people's thinking is controlled by the sinful self, there is death. But if their thinking is controlled by the Spirit, there is life and peace.

Romans 8:6

When you lie down, you won't be afraid; when you lie down, you will sleep in peace.

Proverbs 3:24

We who have believed are able to enter and have God's rest. As God has said, "I was angry and made a promise, 'They will never enter my rest.'" But God's work was finished from the time he made the world. This shows that the rest for God's people is still coming.

Hebrews 4:3, 9

Those who love your teachings will find true peace, and nothing will defeat them.

Psalm 119:165

Those who go to God Most High for safety will be protected by the Almighty. I will say to the LORD, "You are my place of safety and protection. You are my God and I trust you."

Psalm 91:1–2

I leave you peace; my peace I give you. I do not give it to you as the world does. So don't let your hearts be troubled or afraid.

John 14:27

Lonely

Keep your lives free from the love of money, and be satisfied with what you have. God has said, "I will never leave you; I will never forget you."

Hebrews 13:5

Teach them to obey everything that I have taught you, and I will be with you always, even until the end of this age.

Matthew 28:20

For his own sake, the LORD won't leave his people. Instead, he was pleased to make you his own people.

1 Samuel 12:22

So don't worry, because I am with you. Don't be afraid, because I am your God. I will make you strong and will help you; I will support you with my right hand that saves you.

Isaiah 41:10

I will not leave you all alone like orphans; I will come back to you.

John 14:18

Jesus said, "Don't let your hearts be troubled. Trust in God, and trust in me."

John 14:1

The everlasting God is your place of safety, and

his arms will hold you up forever. He will force your enemy out ahead of you, saying, "Destroy the enemy!"

Deuteronomy 33:27

He heals the broken hearted and bandages their wounds.

Psalm 147:3

Can anything separate us from the love Christ has for us? Can troubles or problems or sufferings or hunger or nakedness or danger or violent death? As it is written in the Scriptures: "For you we are in danger of death all the time. People think we are worth no more than sheep to be killed." But in all these things we have full victory through God who showed his love for us. Yes, I am sure that neither death, nor life, nor angels, nor ruling spirits, nothing now, nothing in the future, no powers, nothing above us, nothing below us, nor anything else in the whole world will ever be able to separate us from the love of God that is in Christ Jesus our Lord.

Romans 8:35–39

Because the LORD your God is a merciful God. He will not leave you or destroy you. He will not forget the Agreement with your ancestors, which he swore to them.

Deuteronomy 4:31

Be strong and brave. Don't be afraid of them and don't be frightened, because the LORD your God will go with you. He will not leave you or forget you.

Deuteronomy 31:6

If my father and mother leave me, the LORD will take me in.

Psalm 27:10

"The mountains may disappear, and the hills may come to an end, but my love will never disappear; my promise of peace will not come to an end," says the LORD who shows mercy to you.

Isaiah 54:10

Give all your worries to him, because he cares about you.

1 Peter 5:7

God is our protection and our strength. He always helps in times of trouble.

Psalm 46:1

WHAT TO DO WHEN YOU FEEL

Depressed

The LORD hears good people when they cry out to him, and he saves them from all their troubles.

Psalm 34:17

When you pass through the waters, I will be with you. When you cross rivers, you will not drown. When you walk through fire, you will not be burned, nor will the flames hurt you.

Isaiah 43:2

His anger lasts only a moment, but his kindness lasts for a lifetime. Crying may last for a night, but joy comes in the morning.

Psalm 30:5

My friends, do not be surprised at the terrible trouble which now comes to test you. Do not think that something strange is happening to you. But be happy that you are sharing in Christ's sufferings so that you will be happy and full of joy when Christ comes again in glory.

1 Peter 4:12–13

I will give them a crown to replace their ashes, and the oil of gladness to replace their sorrow, and clothes of praise to replace their spirit of sadness. Then they will be called Trees of Goodness, trees planted by the LORD to show his greatness.

Isaiah 61:3

But the people who trust the LORD will become strong again. They will rise up as an eagle in the sky; they will run and not need rest; they will walk and not become tired.

Isaiah 40:31

Praise be to the God and Father of our Lord Jesus Christ. God is the Father who is full of mercy and all comfort. He comforts us every time we have trouble, so when others have trouble, we can comfort them with the same comfort God gives us.

2 Corinthians 1:3–4

Yes, I am sure that neither death, nor life, nor angels, nor ruling spirits, nothing now, nothing in the future, no powers, nothing above us, nothing below us, nor anything else in the whole world will ever be able to separate us from the love of God that is in Christ Jesus our Lord.

Romans 8:38–39

Brothers and sisters, think about the things that are good and worthy of praise. Think about the things that are true and honorable and right and pure and beautiful and respected.

Philippians 4:8

He heals the brokenhearted and bandages their wounds.

Psalm 147:3

So don't worry, because I am with you. Don't be

afraid, because I am your God. I will make you strong and will help you; I will support you with my right hand that saves you.

Isaiah 41:10

Be humble under God's powerful hand so he will lift you up when the right time comes. Give all your worries to him, because he cares about you.

1 Peter 5:6–7

Then Jesus used this story to teach his followers that they should always pray and never lose hope.

Luke 18:1

Nehemiah said, "Go and enjoy good food and sweet drinks. Send some to people who have none, because today is a holy day to the Lord. Don't be sad, because the joy of the LORD will make you strong."

Nehemiah 8:10

The people the LORD has freed will return and enter Jerusalem with joy. Their happiness will last forever. They will have joy and gladness, and all sadness and sorrow will be gone far away.

Isaiah 51:11

Dissatisfied

Even lions may get weak and hungry, but those who look to the LORD will have every good thing.

Psalm 34:10

I will pour out water for the thirsty land and make streams flow on dry land. I will pour out my Spirit into your children and my blessing on your descendants.

Isaiah 44:3

Trust the LORD and do good. Live in the land and feed on truth.

Psalm 37:3

I know how to live when I am poor, and I know how to live when I have plenty. I have learned the secret of being happy at any time in everything that happens, when I have enough to eat and when I go hungry, when I have more than I need and when I do not have enough. I can do all things through Christ, because he gives me strength.

Philippians 4:12–13

God, you are my God. I search for you. I thirst for you like someone in a dry, empty land where there is no water. I have seen you in the Temple and have seen your strength and glory. Because your love is better than life, I will praise you. I will praise you as long as I live. I will lift up my hands in prayer to your name. I will be content as if I had eaten the best foods. My lips will sing, and my mouth will praise you.

Psalm 63:1–5

People will be rewarded for what they say, and they will also be rewarded for what they do.

Proverbs 12:14

"And my people will be filled with the good things I give them!" says the LORD.

Jeremiah 31:14

Then you will have plenty to eat and be full. You will praise the name of the LORD your God, who has done miracles for you. My people will never again be shamed.

Joel 2:26

My whole being, praise the LORD; all my being, praise his holy name. My whole being, praise the LORD and do not forget all his kindnesses. He forgives all my sins and heals all my diseases. He saves my life from the grave and loads me with love and mercy. He satisfies me with good things and makes me young again, like the eagle.

Psalm 103:1–5

He satisfies the thirsty and fills up the hungry.

Psalm 107:9

God is the one who saves me; I will trust him and not be afraid. The LORD, the LORD gives me strength and makes me sing. He has saved me. You will receive your salvation with joy as you would draw water from a well.

Isaiah 12:2–3

And God can give you more blessings than you need. Then you will always have plenty of everything—enough to give to every good work.

2 Corinthians 9:8

Why spend your money on something that is not real food? Why work for something that doesn't really satisfy you? Listen closely to me, and you will eat what is good; your soul will enjoy the rich food that satisfies.

Isaiah 55:2

Those who want to do right more than anything else are happy, because God will fully satisfy them.

Matthew 5:6

Guilty

So now, those who are in Christ Jesus are not judged guilty.

Romans 8:1

He has not punished us as our sins should be punished; he has not repaid us for the evil we have done. He has taken our sins away from us as far as the east is from west.

Psalm 103:10, 12

If anyone belongs to Christ, there is a new creation. The old things have gone; everything is made new!

2 Corinthians 5:17

God did not send his Son into the world to judge the world guilty, but to save the world through him. People who believe in God's Son are not judged guilty. Those who do not believe have already been judged guilty, because they have not believed in God's one and only Son.

John 3:17–18

I tell you the truth, whoever hears what I say and believes in the One who sent me has eternal life. That person will not be judged guilty but has already left death and entered life.

John 5:24

I will forgive them for the wicked things they did, and I will not remember their sins anymore.

Hebrews 8:12

I, I am the One who forgives all your sins, for my sake; I will not remember your sins.

Isaiah 43:25

The wicked should stop doing wrong, and they should stop their evil thoughts. They should return to the LORD so he may have mercy on them. They should come to our God, because he will freely forgive them.

Isaiah 55:7

Then I confessed my sins to you and didn't hide my guilt. I said, "I will confess my sins to the LORD," and you forgave my guilt.

Psalm 32:5

But if we confess our sins, he will forgive our sins, because we can trust God to do what is right. He will cleanse us from all the wrongs we have done.

1 John 1:9

Happy is the person whose sins are forgiven, whose wrongs are pardoned.

Psalm 32:1

Then I heard a loud voice in heaven saying: "The salvation and the power and the kingdom of our God and the authority of his Christ have now come. The accuser of our brothers and sisters, who accused them day and night before our God, has been thrown down. And our brothers and sisters defeated him by the blood of the Lamb's death and by the message they preached. They did not love their lives so much that they were afraid of death."

Revelation 12:10–11

Jesus raised up again and asked her, "Woman, where are they? Has no one judged you guilty?" She answered, "No one, sir." Then Jesus said, "I also don't judge you guilty. You may go now, but don't sin anymore."

John 8:10–11

"People will no longer have to teach their neighbors and relatives to know the LORD, because all people will know me, from the least to the most important," says the LORD. "I will forgive them for the wicked things they did, and I will not remember their sins anymore."

Jeremiah 31:34

Let us come near to God with a sincere heart and a sure faith, because we have been made free from a guilty conscience, and our bodies have been washed with pure water.

Hebrews 10:22

Come back to the LORD. Then the people who captured your relatives and children will be kind to them and will let them return to this land. The LORD your God is kind and merciful. He will not turn away from you if you return to him.

2 Chronicles 30:9

WHAT TO DO WHEN YOU FEEL

Confused

God is not a God of confusion but a God of peace.

1 Corinthians 14:33a

God did not give us a spirit that makes us afraid but a spirit of power and love and self-control.

2 Timothy 1:7

Where jealousy and selfishness are, there will be confusion and every kind of evil. But the wisdom that comes from God is first of all pure, then peaceful, gentle, and easy to please. This wisdom is always ready to help those who are troubled and to do good for others. It is always fair and honest. People who work for peace in a peaceful way plant a good crop of right-living.

James 3:16–18

The Lord God helps me, so I will not be ashamed. I will be determined, and I know I will not be disgraced.

Isaiah 50:7

My friends, do not be surprised at the terrible trouble which now comes to test you. Do not think that something strange is happening to you. But be happy that you are sharing in Christ's sufferings so that you will be happy and full of joy when Christ comes again in glory.

1 Peter 4:12–13

But if any of you needs wisdom, you should ask God for it. He is generous and enjoys giving to all people, so he will give you wisdom.

James 1:5

Trust the LORD with all your heart, and don't depend on your own understanding. Remember the LORD in all you do, and he will give you success.

Proverbs 3:5–6

The LORD says, "I will make you wise and show you where to go. I will guide you and watch over you."

Psalm 32:8

Those who love your teachings will find true peace, and nothing will defeat them.

Psalm 119:165

But, God, you will bring down the wicked to the grave. Murderers and liars will live only half a lifetime. But I will trust in you.

Psalm 55:23

When you pass through the waters, I will be with you. When you cross rivers, you will not drown. When you walk through fire, you will not be burned, nor will the flames hurt you.

Isaiah 43:2

He gives strength to those who are tired and more power to those who are weak.

Isaiah 40:29

If you go the wrong way— to the right or to the left— you will hear a voice behind you saying, "This is the right way. You should go this way."

Isaiah 30:21

Do not worry about anything, but pray and ask God for everything you need, always giving thanks. And God's peace, which is so great we cannot understand it, will keep your hearts and minds in Christ Jesus.

Philippians 4:6–7

WHAT TO DO WHEN YOU FEEL

Tempted

If you think you are strong, you should be careful not to fall. The only temptation that has come to you is that which everyone has. But you can trust God, who will not permit you to be tempted more than you can stand. But when you are tempted, he will also give you a way to escape so that you will be able to stand it.

1 Corinthians 10:12–13

Since we have a great high priest, Jesus the Son of God, who has gone into heaven, let us hold on to the faith we have. For our high priest is able to understand our weaknesses. When he lived on earth, he was tempted in every way that we are, but he did not sin. Let us, then, feel very sure that we can come before God's throne where there is grace. There we can receive mercy and grace to help us when we need it.

Hebrews 4:14–16

And now he can help those who are tempted, because he himself suffered and was tempted.

Hebrews 2:18

So the Lord knows how to save those who serve him when troubles come. . . .

2 Peter 2:9a

Sin will not be your master, because you are not under law but under God's grace.

Romans 6:14

I have taken your words to heart so I would not sin against you.

Psalm 119:11

When people are tempted, they should not say, "God is tempting me." Evil cannot tempt God, and God himself does not tempt anyone. But people are tempted when their own evil desire leads them away and traps them.

James 1:13–14

If you hide your sins, you will not succeed. If you confess and reject them, you will receive mercy.

Proverbs 28:13

But if we confess our sins, he will forgive our sins, because we can trust God to do what is right. He will cleanse us from all the wrongs we have done.

1 John 1:9

Control yourselves and be careful! The devil, your enemy, goes around like a roaring lion looking for someone to eat. Refuse to give in to him, by standing strong in your faith. You know that your Christian family all over the world is having the same kinds of suffering.

1 Peter 5:8–9

Finally, be strong in the Lord and in his great power. Put on the full armor of God so that you can fight against the devil's evil tricks And also use the shield of faith with which you can stop all the burning arrows of the Evil One.

Ephesians 6:10–11, 16

So give yourselves completely to God. Stand against the devil, and the devil will run from you.

James 4:7

My dear children, you belong to God and have defeated them; because God's Spirit, who is in you, is greater than the devil, who is in the world.

1 John 4:4

My brothers and sisters, when you have many kinds of troubles, you should be full of joy, because you know that these troubles test your faith, and this will give you patience. When people are tempted and still continue strong, they should be happy. After they have proved their faith, God will reward them with life forever. God promised this to all those who love him.

James 1:2–3, 12

God is strong and can help you not to fall. He can bring you before his glory without any wrong in you and can give you great joy. He is the only God, the One who saves us. To him be glory, greatness, power, and authority through Jesus Christ our Lord for all time past, now, and forever. Amen.

Jude 24–25

This makes you very happy, even though now for a short time different kinds of troubles may make you sad. These troubles come to prove that your faith is pure. This purity of faith is worth more than gold, which can be proved to be pure by fire but will ruin. But the purity of your faith will bring you praise and glory and honor when Jesus Christ is shown to you.

1 Peter 1:6–7

WHAT TO DO WHEN YOU FEEL

Angry

My dear brothers and sisters, always be willing to listen and slow to speak. Do not become angry easily, because anger will not help you live the right kind of life God wants.

James 1:19–20

When you are angry, do not sin, and be sure to stop being angry before the end of the day.

Ephesians 4:26

A gentle answer will calm a person's anger, but an unkind answer will cause more anger.

Proverbs 15:1

Yes, if you forgive others for their sins, your Father in heaven will also forgive you for your sins.

Matthew 6:14

Patient people have great understanding, but people with quick tempers show their foolishness.

Proverbs 14:29

Patience is better than strength. Controlling your temper is better than capturing a city.

Proverbs 16:32

Don't become angry quickly, because getting angry is foolish.

Ecclesiastes 7:9

My friends, do not try to punish others when they wrong you, but wait for God to punish them with his anger. It is written: "I will punish those who do wrong; I will repay them," says the Lord.

Romans 12:19

If your enemy is hungry, feed him. If he is thirsty, give him a drink. Doing this will be like pouring burning coals on his head, and the LORD will reward you.

Proverbs 25:21–22

We know that God said, "I will punish those who do wrong; I will repay them." And he also said, "The Lord will judge his people."

Hebrews 10:30

Do not be bitter or angry or mad. Never shout angrily or say things to hurt others. Never do anything evil. Be kind and loving to each other, and forgive each other just as God forgave you in Christ.

Ephesians 4:31–32

But I tell you, if you are angry with a brother or sister, you will be judged. If you say bad things to a brother or sister, you will be judged by the council. And if you call someone a fool, you will be in danger of the fire of hell. So when you offer your gift to God at the altar, and you remember that your brother or sister has something against you, leave your gift there at the altar. Go and make peace with that person, and then come and offer your gift.

Matthew 5:22–24

Wise people are careful and stay out of trouble, but fools are careless and quick to act. Someone with a quick temper does foolish things, but someone with understanding remains calm.

Proverbs 14:16–17

But now also put these things out of your life: anger, bad temper, doing or saying things to hurt others, and using evil words when you talk.

Colossians 3:8

Don't get angry. Don't be upset; it only leads to trouble.

Psalm 37:8

WHAT TO DO WHEN YOU FEEL

Rebellious

Obey your leaders and act under their authority. They are watching over you, because they are responsible for your souls. Obey them so that they will do this work with joy, not sadness. It will not help you to make their work hard.

Hebrews 13:17

Wise people are careful and stay out of trouble, but fools are careless and quick to act. Someone with a quick temper does foolish things, but someone with understanding remains calm.

Proverbs 14:16–17

But Samuel answered, "What pleases the Lord more: burnt offerings and sacrifices or obedience to his voice? It is better to obey than to sacrifice. It is better to listen to God than to offer the fat of sheep. Disobedience is as bad as the sin of sorcery. Pride is as bad as the sin of worshiping idols. You have rejected the Lord's command. Now he rejects you as king."

1 Samuel 15:22–23

So prepare your minds for service and have self-control. All your hope should be for the gift of grace that will be yours when Jesus Christ is shown to you. Now that you are obedient children of God do not live as you did in the past. You did not understand, so you did the evil things you wanted.

1 Peter 1:13–14

"If you become willing and obey me, you will eat good crops from the land. But if you refuse to obey and if you turn against me, you will be destroyed by your enemies' swords." The LORD himself said these things.

Isaiah 1:19–20

For the Lord's sake, yield to the people who have authority in this world: the king, who is the highest authority, and the leaders who are sent by him to punish those who do wrong and to praise those who do right. It is God's desire that by doing good you should stop foolish people from saying stupid things about you.

1 Peter 2:13–15

In your lives you must think and act like Christ Jesus. Christ himself was like God in everything. But he did not think that being equal with God was something to be used for his own benefit. But he gave up his place with God and made himself nothing. He was born to be a man and became like a servant. And when he was living as a man, he humbled himself and was fully obedient to God, even when that caused his death— death on a cross.

Philippians 2:5–8

Even though Jesus was the Son of God, he learned obedience by what he suffered.

Hebrews 5:8

In the same way, younger people should be willing to be under older people. And all of you should be very humble with each other. "God is against the proud, but he gives grace to the humble." Be humble under God's powerful hand so he will lift you up when the right time comes.

1 Peter 5:5–6

Yield to obey each other because you respect Christ.

Ephesians 5:21

No harm comes to a good person, but an evil person's life is full of trouble.

Proverbs 12:21

So, do not let sin control your life here on earth so that you do what your sinful self wants to do. Do not offer the parts of your body to serve sin, as things to be used in doing evil. Instead, offer yourselves to God as people who have died and now live. Offer the parts of your body to God to be used in doing good.

Romans 6:12–13

In the Lord's name, I tell you this. Do not continue living like those who do not believe. Their thoughts are worth nothing. They do not understand, and they know nothing, because they refuse to listen. So they cannot have the life that God gives.

Ephesians 4:17–18

In the past you were full of darkness, but now you are full of light in the Lord. So live like children who belong to the light.

Ephesians 5:8

So give yourselves completely to God. Stand against the devil, and the devil will run from you.

James 4:7

Rejected

But in all these things we have full victory through God who showed his love for us.

Romans 8:37

God does not see the same way people see. People look at the outside of a person, but the LORD looks at the heart.

1 Samuel 16:7b

And you, my son Solomon, accept the God of your father. Serve him completely and willingly, because the LORD knows what is in everyone's mind. He understands everything you think. If you go to him for help, you will get an answer. But if you turn away from him, he will leave you forever.

1 Chronicles 28:9

But if you suffer because you are a Christian, do not be ashamed. Praise God because you wear that name.

1 Peter 4:16

The LORD is close to the brokenhearted, and he saves those whose spirits have been crushed.

Psalm 34:18

Happy are those who don't listen to the wicked, who don't go where sinners go, who don't do what evil people do. They love the LORD's teachings, and they think about those teachings day and night. They are strong, like a tree planted by a river. The tree produces fruit in season, and its leaves don't die. Everything they do will succeed.

Psalm 1:1–3

Those who are treated badly for doing good are happy, because the kingdom of heaven belongs to them.

Matthew 5:10–12

The Father gives me my people. Every one of them will come to me, and I will always accept them.

John 6:37

Depend on the LORD; trust him, and he will take care of you. Then your goodness will shine like the sun, and your fairness like the noonday sun. Wait and trust the LORD. Don't be upset when others get rich or when someone else's plans succeed.

Psalm 37:5–7

God has chosen you and made you his holy people. He loves you. So always do these things: Show mercy to others, be kind, humble, gentle, and patient. Get along with each other, and forgive each other. If someone does wrong to you, forgive that person because the Lord forgave you. Do all these things; but most important, love each other. Love is what holds you all together in perfect unity.

Colossians 3:12–14

What to Do When You Are . . .

Afraid

God did not give us a spirit that makes us afraid but a spirit of power and love and self-control.

2 Timothy 1:7

The Spirit we received does not make us slaves again to fear; it makes us children of God. With that Spirit we cry out, "Father." And the Spirit himself joins with our spirits to say we are God's children.

Romans 8:15–16

Where God's love is, there is no fear, because God's perfect love drives out fear. It is punishment that makes a person fear, so love is not made perfect in the person who fears.

1 John 4:18

Those who go to God Most High for safety will be protected by the Almighty. I will say to the LORD, "You are my place of safety and protection. You are my God and I trust you."

Psalm 91:1–2

But the people who trust the LORD will become strong again. They will rise up as an eagle in the sky; they will run and not need rest; they will walk and not become tired.

Isaiah 40:31

He will cover you with his feathers, and under

his wings you can hide. His truth will be your shield and protection. You will not fear any danger by night or an arrow during the day. You will not be afraid of diseases that come in the dark or sickness that strikes at noon. At your side one thousand people may die, or even ten thousand right beside you, but you will not be hurt.

Psalm 91:4–7

So we can be sure when we say, "I will not be afraid, because the Lord is my helper. People can't do anything to me." Jesus Christ is the same yesterday, today, and forever.

Hebrews 13:6, 8

Nothing bad will happen to you. No disaster will come to your home. He has put his angels in charge of you. They will watch over you wherever you go. The LORD says, "If someone loves me, I will save him."

Psalm 91:10–11, 14

You won't be afraid of sudden trouble; you won't fear the ruin that comes to the wicked, because the LORD will keep you safe. He will keep you from being trapped.

Proverbs 3:25–26

I will build you using fairness. You will be safe from those who would hurt you, so you will have nothing to fear. Nothing will come to make you afraid.

Isaiah 54:14

I trust in God. I will not be afraid. What can people do to me?

Psalm 56:11

Even if I walk through a very dark valley, I will not be afraid, because you are with me. Your rod and your walking stick comfort me You prepare a meal for me in front of my enemies. You pour oil on my head; you fill my cup to overflowing.

Psalm 23:4–5

God knew them before he made the world, and he decided that they would be like his Son so that Jesus would be the firstborn of many brothers. So what should we say about this? If God is with us, no one can defeat us. Can anything separate us from the love Christ has for us? Can troubles or problems or sufferings or hunger or nakedness or danger or violent death? As it is written in the Scriptures: "For you we are in danger of death all the time. People think we are worth no more than sheep to be killed." But in all these things we have full victory through God who showed his love for us. Yes, I am sure that neither death, nor life, nor angels, nor ruling spirits, nothing now, nothing in the future, no powers, nothing above us, nothing below us, nor anything else in the whole world will ever be able to separate us from the love of God that is in Christ Jesus our Lord.

Romans 8:29, 31, 35–39

All you who put your hope in the Lord be strong and brave.

Psalm 31:24

I leave you peace; my peace I give you. I do not give it to you as the world does. So don't let your hearts be troubled or afraid.

John 14:27

The Lord is my light and the one who saves me. I fear no one. The Lord protects my life; I am afraid of no one. If an army surrounds me, I will not be afraid. If war breaks out, I will trust the Lord.

Psalm 27:1, 3

WHAT TO DO WHEN YOU ARE

In Doubt about Yourself

So don't worry, because I am with you. Don't be afraid, because I am your God. I will make you strong and will help you; I will support you with my right hand that saves you.

Isaiah 41:10

God is not a God of confusion but a God of peace. . . .

1 Corinthians 14:33a

Where jealousy and selfishness are, there will be confusion and every kind of evil. But the wisdom that comes from God is first of all pure, then peaceful, gentle, and easy to please. This wisdom is always ready to help those who are troubled and to do good for others. It is always fair and honest. People who work for peace in a peaceful way plant a good crop of right-living.

James 3:16–18

The Scripture says: "I will put a stone in the ground in Jerusalem. Everything will be built on this important and precious rock. Anyone who trusts in him will never be disappointed."

1 Peter 2:6

The Lord GOD helps me, so I will not be ashamed. I will be determined, and I know I will not be disgraced.

Isaiah 50:7

Give your worries to the LORD, and he will take care of you. He will never let good people down. But, God, you will bring down the wicked to the grave. Murderers and liars will live only half a lifetime. But I will trust in you.

Psalm 55:22–23

Do not worry about anything, but pray and ask God for everything you need, always giving thanks. And God's peace, which is so great we cannot understand it, will keep your hearts and minds in Christ Jesus. Brothers and sisters, think about the things that are good and worthy of praise. Think about the things that are true and honorable and right and pure and beautiful and respected.

Philippians 4:6–8

Happy are those who do right, who do what is fair at all times.

Psalm 106:3

Trust the LORD with all your heart, and don't depend on your own understanding. Remember the LORD in all you do, and he will give you success.

Proverbs 3:5–6

Where there is no word from God, people are uncontrolled, but those who obey what they have been taught are happy.

Proverbs 29:18

When you talk, do not say harmful things, but say what people need—words that will help others become stronger. Then what you say will do good to those who listen to you.

Ephesians 4:29

Do to others what you would want them to do to you.

Luke 6:31

Those who love your teachings will find true peace, and nothing will defeat them.

Psalm 119:165

His anger lasts only a moment, but his kindness lasts for a lifetime. Crying may last for a night, but joy comes in the morning.

Psalm 30:5

When you pass through the waters, I will be with you. When you cross rivers, you will not drown. When you walk through fire, you will not be burned, nor will the flames hurt you.

Isaiah 43:2

He heals the brokenhearted and bandages their wounds.

Psalm 147:3

Praise be to the God and Father of our Lord Jesus Christ. God is the Father who is full of mercy and all comfort. He comforts us every time we have trouble, so when others have trouble, we can comfort them with the same comfort God gives us.

2 Corinthians 1:3–4

Yes, I am sure that neither death, nor life, nor angels, nor ruling spirits, nothing now, nothing in the future, no powers, nothing above us, nothing below us, nor anything else in the whole world will ever be able to separate us from the love of God that is in Christ Jesus our Lord.

Romans 8:38–39

As a tree gives fruit, healing words give life; but dishonest words crush the spirit.

Proverbs 15:4

Those who are careful about what they say keep themselves out of trouble.

Proverbs 21:23

You are God's children whom he loves, so try to be like him. Live a life of love just as Christ loved us and gave himself for us as a sweet-smelling offering and sacrifice to God. But there must be no sexual sin among you, or any kind of evil or greed. Those things are not right for God's holy people. Also, there must be no evil talk among you, and you must not speak foolishly or tell evil jokes. These things are not right for you. Instead, you should be giving thanks to God.

Ephesians 5:1–4

WHAT TO DO WHEN YOU ARE

Frantic and Stressed

But the Spirit produces the fruit of love, joy, peace, patience, kindness, goodness, faithfulness, gentleness, self-control. There is no law that says these things are wrong.

Galatians 5:22–23

Wait for the LORD's help. Be strong and brave, and wait for the LORD's help.

Psalm 27:14

The LORD is good to those who hope in him, to those who seek him. It is good to wait quietly for the LORD to save.

Lamentations 3:25–26

But we are hoping for something we do not have yet, and we are waiting for it patiently. Also, the Spirit helps us with our weakness. We do not know how to pray as we should. But the Spirit himself speaks to God for us, even begs God for us with deep feelings that words cannot explain.

Romans 8:25–26

We do not want you to become lazy. Be like those who through faith and patience will receive what God has promised.

Hebrews 6:12

Be joyful because you have hope. Be patient when trouble comes, and pray at all times.

Romans 12:12

Always be humble, gentle, and patient, accepting each other in love.

Ephesians 4:2

Everything that was written in the past was written to teach us. The Scriptures give us patience and encouragement so that we can have hope. Patience and encouragement come from God. And I pray that God will help you all agree with each other the way Christ Jesus wants.

Romans 15:4–5

So do not lose the courage you had in the past, which has a great reward. You must hold on, so you can do what God wants and receive what he has promised.

Hebrews 10:35–36

We have around us many people whose lives tell us what faith means. So let us run the race that is before us and never give up. We should remove from our lives anything that would get in the way and the sin that so easily holds us back.

Hebrews 12:1

It is better to finish something than to start it. It is better to be patient than to be proud. Don't become angry quickly, because getting angry is foolish.

Ecclesiastes 7:8–9

We ask you, brothers and sisters, to warn those who do not work. Encourage the people who are afraid. Help those who are weak. Be patient with everyone.

1 Thessalonians 5:14

Wait and trust the LORD. Don't be upset when others get rich or when someone else's plans succeed. Don't get angry. Don't be upset; it only leads to trouble. It is better to have little and be right than to have much and be wrong.

Psalm 37:7–8, 16

I waited patiently for the LORD. He turned to me and heard my cry.

Psalm 40:1

We also have joy with our troubles, because we know that these troubles produce patience. And patience produces character, and character produces hope. And this hope will never disappoint us, because God has poured out his love to fill our hearts. He gave us his love through the Holy Spirit, whom God has given to us.

Romans 5:3–5

My brothers and sisters, when you have many kinds of troubles, you should be full of joy, because you know that these troubles test your faith, and this will give you patience. Let your patience show itself perfectly in what you do. Then you will be perfect and complete and will have everything you need.

James 1:2–4

Brothers and sisters, be patient until the Lord comes again. A farmer patiently waits for his valuable crop to grow from the earth and for it to receive the autumn and spring rains. You, too, must be patient. Do not give up hope, because the Lord is coming soon.

James 5:7–8

WHAT TO DO WHEN YOU ARE

Unhappy

You, LORD, give true peace to those who depend on you, because they trust you. So, trust the LORD always, because he is our Rock forever.

Isaiah 26:3–4

I leave you peace; my peace I give you. I do not give it to you as the world does. So don't let your hearts be troubled or afraid.

John 14:27

Do not worry about anything, but pray and ask God for everything you need, always giving thanks. And God's peace, which is so great we cannot understand it, will keep your hearts and minds in Christ Jesus.

Philippians 4:6–7

Since we have been made right with God by our faith, we have peace with God. This happened through our Lord Jesus Christ, who has brought us into that blessing of God's grace that we now enjoy. And we are happy because of the hope we have of sharing God's glory.

Romans 5:1–2

He will destroy death forever. The Lord GOD will wipe away every tear from every face. He will take away the shame of his people from the earth. The LORD has spoken. At that time people will say, "Our

God is doing this! We have waited for him, and he has come to save us. This is the LORD. We waited for him, so we will rejoice and be happy when he saves us."

Isaiah 25:8–9

The LORD says, "My thoughts are not like your thoughts. Your ways are not like my ways. Just as the heavens are higher than the earth, so are my ways higher than your ways and my thoughts higher than your thoughts. So you will go out with joy and be led out in peace. The mountains and hills will burst into song before you, and all the trees in the fields will clap their hands."

Isaiah 55:8–9, 12

The LORD saves good people; he is their strength in times of trouble. The LORD helps them and saves them; he saves them from the wicked, because they trust in him for protection.

Psalm 37:39–40

When people's thinking is controlled by the sinful self, they are against God, because they refuse to obey God's law and really are not even able to obey God's law. Those people who are ruled by their sinful selves cannot please God. But you are not ruled by your sinful selves. You are ruled by the Spirit, if that Spirit of God really lives in you. But the person who does not have the Spirit of Christ does not belong to Christ.

Romans 8:7–9

Those who love your teachings will find true peace, and nothing will defeat them. I am waiting for you to save me, Lord. I will obey your commands. I obey your rules, and I love them very much. I obey your orders and rules, because you know everything I do. Hear my cry to you, Lord. Let your word help me understand.

Psalm 119:165–169

"I will give peace, real peace, to those far and near, and I will heal them," says the Lord. But evil people are like the angry sea, which cannot rest, whose waves toss up waste and mud. "There is no peace for evil people," says my God.

Isaiah 57:19–21

The power of the wicked will be broken, but the Lord supports those who do right. The Lord watches over the lives of the innocent, and their reward will last forever. They will not be ashamed when trouble comes. They will be full in times of hunger.

Psalm 37:17–19

God once said, "Let the light shine out of the darkness!" This is the same God who made his light shine in our hearts by letting us know the glory of God that is in the face of Christ. We have troubles all around us, but we are not defeated. We do not know what to do, but we do not give up the hope of living. We are persecuted, but God does not leave us. We are hurt sometimes, but we are not destroyed.

2 Corinthians 4:6, 8–9

I pray that the God who gives hope will fill you with much joy and peace while you trust in him. Then your hope will overflow by the power of the Holy Spirit.

Romans 15:13

In the kingdom of God, eating and drinking are not important. The important things are living right with God, peace, and joy in the Holy Spirit. Anyone who serves Christ by living this way is pleasing God and will be accepted by other people. So let us try to do what makes peace and helps one another.

Romans 14:17–19

Walking Far from God

Wake up! Make yourselves stronger before what you have left dies completely. I have found that what you are doing is less than what my God wants. I know what you do, that you are not hot or cold. I wish that you were hot or cold! But because you are lukewarm— neither hot, nor cold—I am ready to spit you out of my mouth. I correct and punish those whom I love. So be eager to do right, and change your hearts and lives.

Revelation 3:2, 15–16, 19

But I have this against you: You have left the love you had in the beginning. So remember where you were before you fell. Change your hearts and do what you did at first. If you do not change, I will come to you and will take away your lampstand from its place. Every person who has ears should listen to what the Spirit says to the churches. To those who win the victory I will give the right to eat the fruit from the tree of life, which is in the garden of God.

Revelation 2:4–5, 7

Come back to the Lord and say these words to him: "Take away all our sin and kindly receive us, and we will keep the promises we made to you." The Lord says, "I will forgive them for leaving me and will love them freely, because I am not angry with them anymore." A wise person will know these things, and an understanding person will take them to heart. The Lord's ways are right. Good people live by following them, but those who turn against God die because of them.

Hosea 14:2, 4, 9

Don't add to these commands, and don't leave anything out, but obey the commands of the Lord your God that I give you. Obey these laws carefully, in order to show the other nations that you have wisdom and understanding. When they hear about these laws, they will say, "This great nation of Israel is wise and understanding." But be careful! Watch out and don't forget the things you have seen. Don't forget them as long as you live, but teach them to your children and grandchildren.

Deuteronomy 4:2, 6, 9

Do not change yourselves to be like the people of this world, but be changed within by a new way of thinking. Then you will be able to decide what God wants for you; you will know what is good and pleasing to him and what is perfect.

Romans 12:2

Innocent people will be kept safe, but those who are dishonest will suddenly be ruined.

Proverbs 28:18

The honest person will live in safety, but the dishonest will be caught. The words of a good person give life, like a fountain of water, but the words of the wicked contain nothing but violence.

Proverbs 10:9, 11

But if we confess our sins, he will forgive our sins, because we can trust God to do what is right. He will cleanse us from all the wrongs we have done. If we say we have not sinned, we make God a liar, and we do not accept God's teaching.

1 John 1:9–10

Know in your heart that the LORD your God corrects you as a parent corrects a child. Obey the commands of the LORD your God, living as he has commanded you and respecting him. Be careful not to forget the LORD your God so that you fail to obey his commands, laws, and rules that I am giving to you today. If you ever forget the LORD your God and follow other gods and worship them and bow down to them, I warn you today that you will be destroyed.

Deuteronomy 8:5–6, 11, 19

If we had forgotten our God or lifted our hands in prayer to foreign gods, God would have known, because he knows what is in our hearts.

Psalm 44:20–21

So brothers and sisters, be careful that none of you has an evil, unbelieving heart that will turn you away from the living God. But encourage each other every day while it is "today." Help each other so none of you will become hardened because sin has tricked you.

Hebrews 3:12–13

We have much to say about this, but it is hard to explain because you are so slow to understand. By now you should be teachers, but you need someone to teach you again the first lessons of God's message. You still need the teaching that is like milk. You are not ready for solid food.

Hebrews 5:11–12

Be careful that no one fails to receive God's grace and begins to cause trouble among you. A person like that can ruin many of you.

Hebrews 12:15

They were made free from the evil in the world by knowing our Lord and Savior Jesus Christ. But if they return to evil things and those things control them, then it is worse for them than it was before. Yes, it would be better for them to have never known the right way than to know it and to turn away from the holy teaching that was given to them.

2 Peter 2:20–21

This is what the LORD says: "Stand where the roads cross and look. Ask where the old way is, where the good way is, and walk on it. If you do, you will find rest for yourselves. But they have said, 'We will not walk on the good way.'"

Jeremiah 6:16

"Since the time of your ancestors, you have disobeyed my rules and have not kept them. Return to me, and I will return to you," says the LORD All-Powerful. "But you ask, 'How can we return?'"

Malachi 3:7

Uncertain about God

Jesus answered, "Have faith in God. I tell you the truth, you can say to this mountain, 'Go, fall into the sea.' And if you have no doubts in your mind and believe that what you say will happen, God will do it for you. So I tell you to believe that you have received the things you ask for in prayer, and God will give them to you. When you are praying, if you are angry with someone, forgive him so that your Father in heaven will also forgive your sins."

Mark 11:22-25

Don't always think about what you will eat or what you will drink, and don't keep worrying. All the people in the world are trying to get these things, and your Father knows you need them. But seek God's kingdom, and all the other things you need will be given to you.

Luke 12:29–31

Abraham was almost a hundred years old, much past the age for having children, and Sarah could not have children. Abraham thought about all this, but his faith in God did not become weak.

Romans 4:19–21

From the beginning I told you what would happen in the end. A long time ago I told you things that have not yet happened. When I plan something, it happens. What I want to do, I will do. I will make what I have said come true; I will do what I have planned.

Isaiah 46:10–11b

Now may God himself, the God of peace, make you pure, belonging only to him. May your whole self—spirit, soul, and body—be kept safe and without fault when our Lord Jesus Christ comes. You can trust the One who calls you to do that for you.

1 Thessalonians 5:23–24

The Lord is not slow in doing what he promised the way some people understand slowness. But God is being patient with you. He does not want anyone to be lost, but he wants all people to change their hearts and lives.

2 Peter 3:9

The ways of God are without fault. The Lord's words are pure. He is a shield to those who trust him. Who is God? Only the Lord. Who is the Rock? Only our God. God is my protection. He makes my way free from fault. You give me a better way to live, so I live as you want me to.

Psalm 18:30–32, 36

My friends, do not be surprised at the terrible trouble which now comes to test you. Do not think that something strange is happening to you. But be happy that you are sharing in Christ's sufferings so that you will be happy and full of joy when Christ comes again in glory. When people insult you because you follow Christ, you are blessed, because the glorious Spirit, the Spirit of God, is with you.

1 Peter 4:12–14

So faith comes from hearing the Good News, and people hear the Good News when someone tells them about Christ.

Romans 10:17

Come to me and listen; listen to me so you may live. I will make an agreement with you that will last forever. I will give you the blessings I promised to David. So you should look for the LORD before it is too late; you should call to him while he is near. Rain and snow fall from the sky and don't return without watering the ground. They cause the plants to sprout and grow, making seeds for the farmer and bread for the people. The same thing is true of the words I speak. They will not return to me empty. They make the things happen that I want to happen, and they succeed in doing what I send them to do.

Isaiah 55:3, 6, 10–11

"The mountains may disappear, and the hills may come to an end, but my love will never disappear; my promise of peace will not come to an end," says the LORD who shows mercy to you.

Isaiah 54:10

What to Do When . . .

You Don't Feel Important

I can do all things through Christ, because he gives me strength.

Philippians 4:13

So we can be sure when we say, "I will not be afraid, because the Lord is my helper. People can't do anything to me."

Hebrews 13:6

So do not lose the courage you had in the past, which has a great reward. You must hold on, so you can do what God wants and receive what he has promised.

Hebrews 10:35–36

God began doing a good work in you, and I am sure he will continue it until it is finished when Jesus Christ comes again.

Philippians 1:6

And I pray that you and all God's holy people will have the power to understand the greatness of Christ's love—how wide and how long and how high and how deep that love is. Christ's love is greater than anyone can ever know, but I pray that you will be able to know that love. Then you can be filled with the fullness of God.

Ephesians 3:18–19

You were taught to leave your old self—to stop

living the evil way you lived before. That old self becomes worse, because people are fooled by the evil things they want to do. But you were taught to be made new in your hearts.

Ephesians 4:22–23

Also, the Spirit helps us with our weakness. We do not know how to pray as we should. But the Spirit himself speaks to God for us, even begs God for us with deep feelings that words cannot explain. God can see what is in people's hearts. And he knows what is in the mind of the Spirit, because the Spirit speaks to God for his people in the way God wants.

Romans 8:26–27

My whole being, praise the Lord and do not forget all his kindnesses. He forgives all my sins and heals all my diseases.

Psalm 103:2–3

But the people who trust the Lord will become strong again. They will rise up as an eagle in the sky; they will run and not need rest; they will walk and not become tired.

Isaiah 40:31

And this is the boldness we have in God's presence: that if we ask God for anything that agrees with what he wants, he hears us. If we know he hears us every time we ask him, we know we have what we ask from him.

1 John 6:14–15

Then he told me, "This is the word of the LORD to Zerubbabel: 'You will not succeed by your own strength or power, but by my Spirit,' says the LORD All-Powerful."

Zechariah 4:6

When you pass through the waters, I will be with you. When you cross rivers, you will not drown. When you walk through fire, you will not be burned, nor will the flames hurt you.

Isaiah 43:2

You won't be afraid of sudden trouble; you won't fear the ruin that comes to the wicked, because the LORD will keep you safe. He will keep you from being trapped.

Proverbs 3:25–26

In Christ we can come before God with freedom and without fear. We can do this through faith in Christ.

Ephesians 3:12

My dear friends, if our hearts do not make us feel guilty, we can come without fear into God's presence.

1 John 3:21

I tell you the truth, whoever believes in me will do the same things that I do. Those who believe will do even greater things than these, because I am going to the Father.

John 14:12

WHAT TO DO WHEN
Troubles Hit Your Life

The LORD is good, giving protection in times of trouble. He knows who trusts in him.

Nahum 1:7

We have troubles all around us, but we are not defeated. We do not know what to do, but we do not give up the hope of living. We are persecuted, but God does not leave us. We are hurt sometimes, but we are not destroyed.

2 Corinthians 4:8–9

LORD, even when I have trouble all around me, you will keep me alive. When my enemies are angry, you will reach down and save me by your power.

Psalm 138:7

Jesus said, "Don't let your hearts be troubled. Trust in God, and trust in me."

John 14:1

I will guide them along paths they have not known. I will make the darkness become light for them, and the rough ground smooth.

Isaiah 42:16

We know that in everything God works for the good of those who love him. They are the people he called, because that was his plan.

Romans 8:28

I will be glad and rejoice in your love, because you saw my suffering; you knew my troubles.

Psalm 31:7

I look up to the hills, but where does my help come from? My help comes from the LORD, who made heaven and earth.

Psalm 121:1–2

For our high priest is able to understand our weaknesses. When he lived on earth, he was tempted in every way that we are, but he did not sin. Let us, then, feel very sure that we can come before God's throne where there is grace. There we can receive mercy and grace to help us when we need it.

Hebrews 4:15–16

Give all your worries to him, because he cares about you.

1 Peter 5:7

So don't worry about tomorrow, because tomorrow will have its own worries. Each day has enough trouble of its own.

Matthew 6:34

Praise be to the God and Father of our Lord Jesus Christ. God is the Father who is full of mercy and all comfort. He comforts us every time we have trouble, so when others have trouble, we can comfort them with the same comfort God gives us.

2 Corinthians 1:34

Do not worry about anything, but pray and ask God for everything you need, always giving thanks. And God's peace, which is so great we cannot understand it, will keep your hearts and minds in Christ Jesus.

Philippians 4:6–7

The people the Lord has freed will return and enter Jerusalem with joy. Their happiness will last forever. They will have joy and gladness, and all sadness and sorrow will be gone far away.

Isaiah 51:11

WHAT TO DO WHEN

You Have Physical Sickness

My dear friend, I know your soul is doing fine, and I pray that you are doing well in every way and that your health is good.

3 John 2

Jesus traveled through all the towns and villages, teaching in their synagogues, preaching the Good News about the kingdom, and healing all kinds of diseases and sicknesses.

Matthew 9:35

All the people were trying to touch Jesus, because power was coming from him and healing them all.

Luke 6:19

Jesus Christ is the same yesterday, today, and forever.

Hebrews 13:8

Christ carried our sins in his body on the cross so we would stop living for sin and start living for what is right. And you are healed because of his wounds.

1 Peter 2:24

He forgives all my sins and heals all my diseases.

Psalm 103:3

Anyone who is sick should call the church's elders. They should pray for and pour oil on the person in the name of the LORD. And the prayer that is said with faith will make the sick person well; the LORD will heal that person. And if the person has sinned, the sins will be forgiven.

James 5:14–15

And those who believe will be able to do these things as proof: They will use my name to force out demons. They will speak in new languages. They will pick up snakes and drink poison without being hurt. They will touch the sick, and the sick will be healed.

Mark 16:17–18

But he was wounded for the wrong we did; he was crushed for the evil we did. The punishment, which made us well, was given to him, and we are healed because of his wounds.

Isaiah 53:5

LORD, heal me, and I will truly be healed. Save me, and I will truly be saved. You are the one I praise.

Jeremiah 17:14

"I will bring back your health and heal your injuries," says the LORD. . . .

Jeremiah 30:17a

He said, "You must obey the LORD your God and do what he says is right. If you obey all his commands and keep his rules, I will not bring on you any of the sicknesses I brought on the Egyptians. I am the LORD who heals you."

Exodus 15:26

My child, pay attention to my words; listen closely to what I say. Don't ever forget my words; keep them always in mind. They are the key to life for those who find them; they bring health to the whole body.

Proverbs 4:20–22

God gave the command and healed them, so they were saved from dying.

Psalm 107:20

The officer answered, "Lord, I am not worthy for you to come into my house. You only need to command it, and my servant will be healed."

Matthew 8:8

You Need Money

Those who work hard make a profit, but those who only talk will be poor.

Proverbs 14:23

When a person's steps follow the LORD, God is pleased with his ways. If he stumbles, he will not fall, because the LORD holds his hand. I was young, and now I am old, but I have never seen good people left helpless or their children begging for food.

Psalm 37:23–25

Even lions may get weak and hungry, but those who look to the LORD will have every good thing.

Psalm 34:10

The LORD is my shepherd; I have everything I need.

Psalm 23:1

Obey the LORD your God so that all these blessings will come and stay with you: You will be blessed in the city and blessed in the country. Your children will be blessed, as well as your crops; your herds will be blessed with calves and your flocks with lambs. Your basket and your kitchen will be blessed. You will be blessed when you come in and when you go out. The LORD will help you defeat the enemies that come to fight you. They will attack you from one direction, but they will run from you in seven directions. The

Lord your God will bless you with full barns, and he will bless everything you do. He will bless the land he is giving you.

Deuteronomy 28:2–8

The Lord will make you rich: You will have many children, your animals will have many young, and your land will give good crops. It is the land that the Lord promised your ancestors he would give to you. The Lord will open up his heavenly storehouse so that the skies send rain on your land at the right time, and he will bless everything you do. You will lend to other nations, but you will not need to borrow from them. The Lord will make you like the head and not like the tail; you will be on top and not on bottom. But you must obey the commands of the Lord your God that I am giving you today, being careful to keep them.

Deuteronomy 28:11–13

The Lord your God is bringing you into a good land, a land with rivers and pools of water, with springs that flow in the valleys and hills, a land that has wheat and barley, vines, fig trees, pomegranates, olive oil, and honey. It is a land where you will have plenty of food, where you will have everything you need, where the rocks are iron, and where you can dig copper out of the hills. When you have all you want to eat, then praise the Lord your God for giving you a good land. Be careful not to forget the Lord your God so that you fail to obey his commands, laws, and rules that I am giving to you today. When you eat all you want and build nice houses and live in them, when your herds and flocks grow large and your silver and gold increase, when you have more of everything, then your heart will become proud. You will forget the LORD your God, who brought you out of the land of Egypt, where you were slaves. But remember the LORD your God! It is he who gives you the power to become rich, keeping the agreement he promised to your ancestors, as it is today.

Deuteronomy 8:7–14, 18

Don't worry and say, "What will we eat?" or "What will we drink?" or "What will we wear?" The people who don't know God keep trying to get these things, and your Father in heaven knows you need them. The thing you should want most is God's kingdom and doing what God wants. Then all these other things you need will be given to you.

Matthew 6:31–33

If people please God, God will give them wisdom, knowledge, and joy. But sinners will get only the work of gathering and storing wealth that they will have to give to the ones who please God. So all their work is useless, like chasing the wind.

Ecclesiastes 2:26

I know how to live when I am poor, and I know how to live when I have plenty. I have learned the secret of being happy at any time in everything that happens, when I have enough to eat and when I go hungry, when I have more than I need and when I do not have enough. I can do all things through Christ, because he gives me strength.

Philippians 4:12–13

Those who want to become rich bring temptation to themselves and are caught in a trap. They want many foolish and harmful things that ruin and destroy people. The love of money causes all kinds of evil. Some people have left the faith, because they wanted to get more money, but they have caused themselves much sorrow.

1 Timothy 6:9–10

The earth belongs to the Lord, and everything in it—the world and all its people.

Psalm 24:1

Give, and you will receive. You will be given much. Pressed down, shaken together, and running over, it will spill into your lap. The way you give to others is the way God will give to you.

Luke 6:38

On the first day of every week, each one of you should put aside money as you have been blessed. . . .

1 Corinthians 16:2a

Heal the sick, raise the dead to life again, heal those who have skin diseases, and force demons out of people. I give you these powers freely, so help other people freely.

Matthew 10:8

"Bring to the storehouse a full tenth of what you earn so there will be food in my house. Test me in this," says the Lord All-Powerful. "I will open the windows of heaven for you and pour out all the blessings you need. I will stop the insects so they won't eat your crops. The grapes won't fall from your vines before they are ready to pick," says the Lord All-Powerful. "All the nations will call you blessed, because you will have a pleasant country," says the Lord All-Powerful.

Malachi 3:10–12

Remember this: The person who plants a little will have a small harvest, but the person who plants a lot will have a big harvest. Each one should give as you have decided in your heart to give. You should not be sad when you give, and you should not give because you feel forced to give. God loves the person who gives happily. And God can give you more blessings than you need. Then you will always have plenty of everything— enough to give to every good work.

2 Corinthians 9:6–8

And all those who have left houses, brothers, sisters, father, mother, children, or farms to follow me will get much more than they left, and they will have life forever.

Matthew 19:29

Always remember what is written in the Book of the Teachings. Study it day and night to be sure to obey everything that is written there. If you do this, you will be wise and successful in everything.

Joshua 1:8

Good people leave their wealth to their grandchildren, but a sinner's wealth is stored up for good people.

Proverbs 13:22

My God will use his wonderful riches in Christ Jesus to give you everything you need.

Philippians 4:19

No one can serve two masters. The person will hate one master and love the other, or will follow one master and refuse to follow the other. You cannot serve both God and worldly riches. So I tell you, don't worry about the food or drink you need to live, or about the clothes you need for your body. Life is more than food, and the body is more than clothes.

Matthew 6:24–25

No one has ever given me anything that I must pay back, because everything under the sky belongs to me.

Job 41:11

Command those who are rich with things of this world not to be proud. Tell them to hope in God, not in their uncertain riches. God richly gives us everything to enjoy. Tell the rich people to do good, to be rich in doing good deeds, to be generous and ready to share. By doing that, they will be saving a treasure for themselves as a strong foundation for the future. Then they will be able to have the life that is true life.

1 Timothy 6:17–19

WHAT TO DO WHEN

Someone Close to You Dies

Brothers and sisters, we want you to know about those Christians who have died so you will not be sad, as others who have no hope. We believe that Jesus died and that he rose again. So, because of him, God will raise with Jesus those who have died.

1 Thessalonians 4:13–14

The Lord comforts his people and will have pity on those who suffer.

Isaiah 49:13b

When you pass through the waters, I will be with you. When you cross rivers, you will not drown. When you walk through fire, you will not be burned, nor will the flames hurt you. This is because I, the Lord, am your God, the Holy One of Israel, your Savior.

Isaiah 43:2–3a

May our Lord Jesus Christ himself and God our Father encourage you and strengthen you in every good thing you do and say. God loved us, and through his grace he gave us a good hope and encouragement that continues forever.

2 Thessalonians 2:16–17

Those who are sad now are happy, because God will comfort them.

Matthew 5:4

Praise be to the God and Father of our Lord Jesus Christ. God is the Father who is full of mercy and all comfort. He comforts us every time we have trouble, so when others have trouble, we can comfort them with the same comfort God gives us. We share in the many sufferings of Christ. In the same way, much comfort comes to us through Christ.

2 Corinthians 1:3–5

The Lord God has put his Spirit in me, because the Lord has appointed me to tell the good news to the poor. He sent me to comfort those whose hearts are broken, to tell the captives they are free, and to tell the prisoners they are released. He has sent me to announce the time when the Lord will show his kindness and the time when our God will punish evil people. He has sent me to comfort all those who are sad and to help the sorrowing people of Jerusalem. I will give them a crown to replace their ashes, and the oil of gladness to replace their sorrow, and clothes of praise to replace their spirit of sadness. Then they will be called Trees of Goodness, trees planted by the Lord to show his greatness.

Isaiah 61:1–3

He will wipe away every tear from their eyes, and there will be no more death, sadness, crying, or pain, because all the old ways are gone.

Revelation 21:4

Lord, show me your love, and save me as you have

promised. When I suffer, this comforts me: Your promise gives me life.

Psalm 119:41, 50

Give all your worries to him, because he cares about you.

1 Peter 5:7

"Death, where is your victory? Death, where is your pain?" Death's power to hurt is sin, and the power of sin is the law. But we thank God! He gives us the victory through our Lord Jesus Christ.

1 Corinthians 15:55–57

Even if I walk through a very dark valley, I will not be afraid, because you are with me. Your rod and your walking stick comfort me.

Psalm 23:4

Since we have a great high priest, Jesus the Son of God, who has gone into heaven, let us hold on to the faith we have. For our high priest is able to understand our weaknesses. When he lived on earth, he was tempted in every way that we are, but he did not sin. Let us, then, feel very sure that we can come before God's throne where there is grace. There we can receive mercy and grace to help us when we need it.

Hebrews 4:14–16

So don't worry, because I am with you. Don't be afraid, because I am your God. I will make you strong and will help you; I will support you with my right hand that saves you.

Isaiah 41:10

The people the LORD has freed will return and enter Jerusalem with joy. Their happiness will last forever. They will have joy and gladness, and all sadness and sorrow will be gone far away.

Isaiah 51:11

So I say that we have courage. We really want to be away from this body and be at home with the Lord. Our only goal is to please God whether we live here or there, because we must all stand before Christ to be judged. Each of us will receive what we should get— good or bad—for the things we did in the earthly body.

2 Corinthians 5:8–10

You Are Deserted

Those who know the LORD trust him, because he
will not leave those who come to him.

Psalm 9:10

The LORD won't leave his people nor give up his
children.

Psalm 94:14

If my father and mother leave me, the LORD will
take me in.

Psalm 27:10

Teach them to obey everything that I have taught
you, and I will be with you always, even until the end
of this age.

Matthew 28:20

You will never again be called the People that God
Left, nor your land the Land that God Destroyed.
You will be called the People God Loves, and your
land will be called the Bride of God, because the Lord
loves you. And your land will belong to him as a bride
belongs to her husband.

Isaiah 62:4

We are persecuted, but God does not leave us. We
are hurt sometimes, but we are not destroyed.

2 Corinthians 4:9

Give all your worries to him, because he cares about you.

1 Peter 5:7

For his own sake, the LORD won't leave his people. Instead, he was pleased to make you his own people.

1 Samuel 12:22

I was young, and now I am old, but I have never seen good people left helpless or their children begging for food.

Psalm 37:25

The LORD your God is a merciful God. He will not leave you or destroy you. He will not forget the Agreement with your ancestors, which he swore to them.

Deuteronomy 4:31

The poor and needy people look for water, but they can't find any. Their tongues are dry with thirst. But I, the LORD, will answer their prayers; I, the God of Israel, will not leave them to die.

Isaiah 41:17

The LORD says, "Whoever loves me, I will save. I will protect those who know me. They will call to me, and I will answer them. I will be with them in trouble; I will rescue them and honor them."

Psalm 91:14–15

"Can a woman forget the baby she nurses? Can she feel no kindness for the child to which she gave birth? Even if she could forget her children, I will not forget you. See, I have written your name on my hand."

Isaiah 49:15–16a

Why am I so sad? Why am I so upset? I should put my hope in God and keep praising him, my Savior and my God.

Psalm 43:5

Be strong and brave. Don't be afraid of them and don't be frightened, because the LORD your God will go with you. He will not leave you or forget you.

Deuteronomy 31:6

You Don't Understand God's Ways

The Lord says, "My thoughts are not like your thoughts. Your ways are not like my ways. Just as the heavens are higher than the earth, so are my ways higher than your ways and my thoughts higher than your thoughts."

Isaiah 55:8–9

Judah, pray to me, and I will answer you. I will tell you important secrets you have never heard before.

Jeremiah 33:3

So what should we say about this? If God is with us, no one can defeat us.

Romans 8:31

Can anything separate us from the love Christ has for us? Can troubles or problems or sufferings or hunger or nakedness or danger or violent death? As it is written in the Scriptures: "For you we are in danger of death all the time. People think we are worth no more than sheep to be killed." But in all these things we have full victory through God who showed his love for us.

Romans 8:35–37

The only temptation that has come to you is that which everyone has. But you can trust God, who will not permit you to be tempted more than you can stand. But when you are tempted, he will also give you a way to escape so that you will be able to stand it.

1 Corinthians 10:13

People who do what is right may have many problems, but the LORD will solve them all.

Psalm 34:19

But, God, you will bring down the wicked to the grave. Murderers and liars will live only half a lifetime. But I will trust in you.

Psalm 55:23

My friends, do not be surprised at the terrible trouble which now comes to test you. Do not think that something strange is happening to you. But be happy that you are sharing in Christ's sufferings so that you will be happy and full of joy when Christ comes again in glory.

1 Peter 4:12–13

So don't worry, because I am with you. Don't be afraid, because I am your God. I will make you strong and will help you; I will support you with my right hand that saves you.

Isaiah 41:10

We know that in everything God works for the good of those who love him. They are the people he called, because that was his plan.

Romans 8:28

Come, let's go back to the Lord. He has hurt us, but he will heal us. He has wounded us, but he will bandage our wounds. In two days he will put new life in us; on the third day he will raise us up so that we may live in his presence and know him. Let's try to learn about the Lord; He will come to us as surely as the dawn comes. He will come to us like rain, like the spring rain that waters the ground.

Hosea 6:1–3

The ways of God are without fault. The Lord's words are pure. He is a shield to those who trust him.

Psalm 18:30

Let us hold firmly to the hope that we have confessed, because we can trust God to do what he promised.

Hebrews 10:23

I will make an agreement with them that will last forever. I will never turn away from them; I will always do good to them. I will make them want to respect me so they will never turn away from me.

Jeremiah 32:40

Lord, you do everything for me. Lord, your love continues forever. Do not leave us, whom you made.

Psalm 138:8

Nothing Seems to Be Going Right

Wait for the LORD's help. Be strong and brave, and wait for the LORD's help.

Psalm 27:14

I find rest in God; only he gives me hope.

Psalm 62:5

So our hope is in the LORD. He is our help, our shield to protect us.

Psalm 33:20

But the people who trust the LORD will become strong again. They will rise up as an eagle in the sky; they will run and not need rest; they will walk and not become tired.

Isaiah 40:31

It is not yet time for the message to come true, but that time is coming soon; the message will come true. It may seem like a long time, but be patient and wait for it, because it will surely come; it will not be delayed.

Habakkuk 2:3

Let us hold firmly to the hope that we have confessed, because we can trust God to do what he promised.

Hebrews 10:23

All living things look to you for food, and you give it to them at the right time. You open your hand, and you satisfy all living things.

Psalm 145:15–16

I wait for the LORD to help me, and I trust his word.

Psalm 130:5

We all share in Christ if we keep till the end the sure faith we had in the beginning.

Hebrews 3:14

At that time people will say, "Our God is doing this! We have waited for him, and he has come to save us. This is the LORD. We waited for him, so we will rejoice and be happy when he saves us."

Isaiah 25:9

Yes, my dear children, live in him so that when Christ comes back, we can be without fear and not be ashamed in his presence.

1 John 2:28

So be very careful how you live. Do not live like those who are not wise, but live wisely.

Ephesians 5:15

In the past you were full of darkness, but now you are full of light in the LORD. So live like children who belong to the light. Light brings every kind of goodness, right living, and truth. Try to learn what pleases the Lord. Have nothing to do with the things done in darkness, which are not worth anything. But show that they are wrong.

Ephesians 5:8–11

Let us live in a right way, like people who belong to the day. We should not have wild parties or get drunk. There should be no sexual sins of any kind, no fighting or jealousy. But clothe yourselves with the Lord Jesus Christ and forget about satisfying your sinful self.

Romans 13:13-14

The Bible Is Your...

THE BIBLE IS YOUR

Dependable Authority

All Scripture is given by God and is useful for teaching, for showing people what is wrong in their lives, for correcting faults, and for teaching how to live right. Using the Scriptures, the person who serves God will be capable, having all that is needed to do every good work.

2 Timothy 3:16–17

Most of all, you must understand this: No prophecy in the Scriptures ever comes from the prophet's own interpretation. No prophecy ever came from what a person wanted to say, but people led by the Holy Spirit spoke words from God.

2 Peter 1:20–21

God's word is alive and working and is sharper than a double-edged sword. It cuts all the way into us, where the soul and the spirit are joined, to the center of our joints and bones. And it judges the thoughts and feelings in our hearts. Nothing in all the world can be hidden from God. Everything is clear and lies open before him, and to him we must explain the way we have lived.

Hebrews 4:12–13

Rain and snow fall from the sky and don't return without watering the ground. They cause the plants to sprout and grow, making seeds for the farmer and bread for the people. The same thing is true of the words I speak. They will not return to me empty. They make the things happen that I want to happen, and they succeed in doing what I send them to do.

Isaiah 55:10–11

And the Father himself who sent me has given proof about me. You have never heard his voice or seen what he looks like. You carefully study the Scriptures because you think they give you eternal life. They do in fact tell about me.

John 5:37, 39

Earth and sky will be destroyed, but the words I have said will never be destroyed.

Mark 13:31

You have been born again, and this new life did not come from something that dies, but from something that cannot die. You were born again through God's living message that continues forever. The Scripture says, "All people are like the grass, and all their glory is like the flowers of the field. The grass dies and the flowers fall, but the word of the Lord will live forever. "And this is the word that was preached to you.

1 Peter 1:23-25

All the earth should worship the Lord; the whole world should fear him. He spoke, and it happened. He commanded, and it appeared.

Psalm 33:8–9

Every word of God is true. He guards those who come to him for safety.

Proverbs 30:5

LORD, your word is everlasting; it continues forever in heaven.

Psalm 119:89

But the LORD's plans will stand forever; his ideas will last from now on. Happy is the nation whose God is the LORD, the people he chose for his very own.

Psalm 33:11–12

The yes to all of God's promises is in Christ, and through Christ we say yes to the glory of God.

2 Corinthians 1:20

Way to Succeed

Now I am putting you in the care of God and the message about his grace. It is able to give you strength, and it will give you the blessings God has for all his holy people.

Acts 20:32

Stand up! I have chosen you to be my servant and my witness—you will tell people the things that you have seen and the things that I will show you. This is why I have come to you today. I am sending you to them to open their eyes so that they may turn away from darkness to the light, away from the power of Satan and to God. Then their sins can be forgiven, and they can have a place with those people who have been made holy by believing in me.

Acts 26:16, 17b–18

The Spirit we received does not make us slaves again to fear; it makes us children of God. With that Spirit we cry out, "Father." And the Spirit himself joins with our spirits to say we are God's children. If we are God's children, we will receive blessings from God together with Christ. But we must suffer as Christ suffered so that we will have glory as Christ has glory.

Romans 8:15–17

In Christ we were chosen to be God's people, because from the very beginning God had decided this in keeping with his plan. And he is the One who makes everything agree with what he decides and wants. We are the first people who hoped in Christ, and we were chosen so that we would bring praise to God's glory. So it is with you. When you heard the true teaching —the Good News about your salvation—you believed in Christ. And in Christ, God put his special mark of ownership on you by giving you the Holy Spirit that he had promised. That Holy Spirit is the guarantee that we will receive what God promised for his people until God gives full freedom to those who are his—to bring praise to God's glory.

Ephesians 1:11–14

You belong to Christ, so you are Abraham's descendants. You will inherit all of God's blessings because of the promise God made to Abraham.

Galatians 3:29

This is that secret: that through the Good News those who are not Jews will share with the Jews in God's blessing. They belong to the same body, and they share together in the promise that God made in Christ Jesus.

Ephesians 3:6

In all the work you are doing, work the best you can. Work as if you were doing it for the Lord, not for people. Remember that you will receive your reward from the Lord, which he promised to his people. You are serving the Lord Christ.

Colossians 3:23–24

There are many rooms in my Father's house; I would not tell you this if it were not true. I am going there to prepare a place for you. After I go and prepare a place for you, I will come back and take you to be with me so that you may be where I am.

John 14:2–3

Then the King will say to the people on his right, "Come, my Father has given you his blessing. Receive the kingdom God has prepared for you since the world was made."

Matthew 25:34

Serving God does make us very rich, if we are satisfied with what we have. We brought nothing into the world, so we can take nothing out. But, if we have food and clothes, we will be satisfied with that. Those who want to become rich bring temptation to themselves and are caught in a trap. They want many foolish and harmful things that ruin and destroy people.

1 Timothy 6:6–9

The yes to all of God's promises is in Christ, and through Christ we say yes to the glory of God. Remember, God is the One who makes you and us strong in Christ. God made us his chosen people.

2 Corinthians 1:20–21

Praise be to the God and Father of our Lord Jesus Christ. In God's great mercy he has caused us to be born again into a living hope, because Jesus Christ rose from the dead. Now we hope for the blessings God has for his children. These blessings, which cannot be destroyed or be spoiled or lose their beauty, are kept in heaven for you.

1 Peter 1:3–4

But as it is written in the Scriptures: "No one has ever seen this, and no one has ever heard about it. No one has ever imagined what God has prepared for those who love him."

1 Corinthians 2:9

Jesus called us by his glory and goodness. Through these he gave us the very great and precious promises. With these gifts you can share in being like God, and the world will not ruin you with its evil desires.

2 Peter 1:3b–4

Wait for the LORD's help and follow him. He will honor you and give you the land, and you will see the wicked sent away.

Psalm 37:34

THE BIBLE IS YOUR
Guide for Life

Your word is like a lamp for my feet and a light for my path.

Psalm 119:105

My son, keep your father's commands, and don't forget your mother's teaching. Keep their words in mind forever as though you had them tied around your neck. They will guide you when you walk. They will guard you when you sleep. They will speak to you when you are awake. These commands are like a lamp; this teaching is like a light. And the correction that comes from them will help you have life.

Proverbs 6:20–23

I have taken your words to heart so I would not sin against you.

Psalm 119:11

The orders of the LORD are right; they make people happy. The commands of the LORD are pure; they light up the way. Respect for the LORD is good; it will last forever. The judgments of the LORD are true; they are completely right. They are worth more than gold, even the purest gold. They are sweeter than honey, even the finest honey. By them your servant is warned. Keeping them brings great reward.

Psalm 19:8–11

How can a young person live a pure life? By obeying your word.

Psalm 119:9

So Jesus said to the Jews who believed in him, "If you continue to obey my teaching, you are truly my followers. Then you will know the truth, and the truth will make you free."

John 8:31–32

All Scripture is given by God and is useful for teaching, for showing people what is wrong in their lives, for correcting faults, and for teaching how to live right. Using the Scriptures, the person who serves God will be capable, having all that is needed to do every good work.

2 Timothy 3:16–17

Your rules give me pleasure; they give me good advice.

Psalm 119:24

Through these he gave us the very great and precious promises. With these gifts you can share in being like God, and the world will not ruin you with its evil desires.

2 Peter 1:4

When a person's steps follow the LORD, God is pleased with his ways. If he stumbles, he will not fall, because the LORD holds his hand.

Psalm 37:23–24

The Lord says, "I will make you wise and show you where to go. I will guide you and watch over you."

Psalm 32:8

He gives me new strength. He leads me on paths that are right for the good of his name.

Psalm 23:3

If you go the wrong way— to the right or to the left— you will hear a voice behind you saying, "This is the right way. You should go this way."

Isaiah 30:21

God promised Abraham, our father, that he would save us from the power of our enemies so we could serve him without fear, being holy and good before God as long as we live.

Luke 1:73–75

Always remember what is written in the Book of the Teachings. Study it day and night to be sure to obey everything that is written there. If you do this, you will be wise and successful in everything.

Joshua 1:8

THE BIBLE IS YOUR

Solid Rock

You have been born again, and this new life did not come from something that dies, but from something that cannot die. You were born again through God's living message that continues forever. The Scripture says, "All people are like the grass, and all their glory is like the flowers of the field. The grass dies and the flowers fall, but the word of the Lord will live forever. "And this is the word that was preached to you.

1 Peter 1:23–25

Earth and sky will be destroyed, but the words I have said will never be destroyed.

Matthew 24:35

LORD, your word is everlasting; it continues forever in heaven.

Psalm 119:89

The grass dies and the flowers fall, but the word of our God will live forever.

Isaiah 40:8

I tell you the truth, nothing will disappear from the law until heaven and earth are gone. Not even the smallest letter or the smallest part of a letter will be lost until everything has happened.

Matthew 5:18

Praise the LORD! He promised he would give rest to his people Israel, and he has given us rest. The LORD has kept all the good promises he gave through his servant Moses.

1 Kings 8:56

God is strong and can help you not to fall. He can bring you before his glory without any wrong in you and can give you great joy. He is the only God, the One who saves us. To him be glory, greatness, power, and authority through Jesus Christ our Lord for all time past, now, and forever. Amen.

Jude 24–25

There will be no more false visions or pleasing prophecies inside the nation of Israel, but I, the LORD, will speak. What I say will be done, and it will not be delayed. You refuse to obey, but in your time I will say the word and do it," says the LORD God.

Ezekiel 12:24–25

My child, pay attention to my words; listen closely to what I say. Don't ever forget my words; keep them always in mind. They are the key to life for those who find them; they bring health to the whole body.

Proverbs 4:20–22

We know that in everything God works for the good of those who love him. They are the people he called, because that was his plan. So what should we say about this? If God is with us, no one can defeat us.

Romans 8:28, 31

The Lord surely loves his people and takes care of all those who belong to him. They bow down at his feet, and they are taught by him. The everlasting God is your place of safety, and his arms will hold you up forever. He will force your enemy out ahead of you, saying, "Destroy the enemy!"

Deuteronomy 33:3, 27

He lifted me out of the pit of destruction, out of the sticky mud. He stood me on a rock and made my feet steady. He put a new song in my mouth, a song of praise to our God. Many people will see this and worship him. Then they will trust the Lord.

Psalm 40:2–3

God is our protection and our strength. He always helps in times of trouble.

Psalm 46:1

The Lord is like a strong tower; those who do right can run to him for safety.

Proverbs 18:10

But the Lord is faithful and will give you strength and will protect you from the Evil One.

2 Thessalonians 3:3

THE BIBLE IS YOUR
Source of Strength

"Master, how can I, your servant, talk with you? My strength is gone, and it is hard for me to breathe." He said, "Daniel, don't be afraid. God loves you very much. Peace be with you. Be strong now; be courageous." When he spoke to me, I became stronger and said, "Master, speak, since you have given me strength."

Daniel 10:17, 19

I am sad and tired. Make me strong again as you have promised.

Psalm 119:28

This is what the Lord GOD, the Holy One of Israel, says: "If you come back to me and trust me, you will be saved. If you will be calm and trust me, you will be strong."

Isaiah 30:15

I ask the Father in his great glory to give you the power to be strong inwardly through his Spirit. I pray that Christ will live in your hearts by faith and that your life will be strong in love and be built on love.

Ephesians 3:16–17

God will strengthen you with his own great power so that you will not give up when troubles come, but you will be patient. And you will joyfully give thanks to the Father who has made you able to have a share in all that he has prepared for his people in the kingdom of light.

Colossians 1:11–12

He gives strength to those who are tired and more power to those who are weak. Even children become tired and need to rest, and young people trip and fall. But the people who trust the LORD will become strong again. They will rise up as an eagle in the sky; they will run and not need rest; they will walk and not become tired.

Isaiah 40:29–31

Nehemiah said, "Go and enjoy good food and sweet drinks. Send some to people who have none, because today is a holy day to the LORD. Don't be sad, because the joy of the LORD will make you strong."

Nehemiah 8:10

I can do all things through Christ, because he gives me strength.

Philippians 4:13

So don't worry, because I am with you. Don't be afraid, because I am your God. I will make you strong and will help you; I will support you with my right hand that saves you.

Isaiah 41:10

I have good sense and advice, and I have understanding and power.

Proverbs 8:14

I love you, LORD. You are my strength. The LORD is my rock, my protection, my Savior. My God is my rock. I can run to him for safety. He is my shield and my saving strength, my defender. I will call to the LORD, who is worthy of praise, and I will be saved from my enemies.

Psalm 18:1–3

That is why you need to put on God's full armor. Then on the day of evil you will be able to stand strong. And when you have finished the whole fight, you will still be standing. So stand strong, with the belt of truth tied around your waist and the protection of right living on your chest.

Ephesians 6:13–14

The LORD is my light and the one who saves me. I fear no one. The LORD protects my life; I am afraid of no one. Evil people may try to destroy my body. My enemies and those who hate me attack me, but they are overwhelmed and defeated.

Psalm 27:1–2

Finally, be strong in the Lord and in his great power.

Ephesians 6:10

*What the Bible Has
to Say about. . .*

WHAT THE BIBLE HAS TO SAY ABOUT
Faith

It is by faith we understand that the whole world was made by God's command so what we see was made by something that cannot be seen.

Hebrews 11:3

So faith comes from hearing the Good News, and people hear the Good News when someone tells them about Christ.

Romans 10:17

Because God has given me a special gift, I have something to say to everyone among you. Do not think you are better than you are. You must decide what you really are by the amount of faith God has given you.

Romans 12:3

We have around us many people whose lives tell us what faith means. So let us run the race that is before us and never give up. We should remove from our lives anything that would get in the way and the sin that so easily holds us back. Let us look only to Jesus, the One who began our faith and who makes it perfect. He suffered death on the cross. But he accepted the shame as if it were nothing because of the joy that God put before him. And now he is sitting at the right side of God's throne.

Hebrews 12:1–2

Jesus answered, "Because your faith is too small. I tell you the truth, if your faith is as big as a mustard seed, you can say to this mountain, 'Move from here to there,' and it will move. All things will be possible for you."

Matthew 17:20

Jesus answered, "Have faith in God. I tell you the truth, you can say to this mountain, 'Go, fall into the sea.' And if you have no doubts in your mind and believe that what you say will happen, God will do it for you. So I tell you to believe that you have received the things you ask for in prayer, and God will give them to you."

Mark 11:22–24

Jesus said to the father, "You said, 'If you can!' All things are possible for the one who believes." Immediately the father cried out, "I do believe! Help me to believe more!"

Mark 9:23–24

The Good News shows how God makes people right with himself—that it begins and ends with faith. As the Scripture says, "But those who are right with God will live by trusting in him."

Romans 1:17

We live by what we believe, not by what we can see.

2 Corinthians 5:7

Without faith no one can please God. Anyone who comes to God must believe that he is real and that he rewards those who truly want to find him.

Hebrews 11:6

These troubles come to prove that your faith is pure. This purity of faith is worth more than gold, which can be proved to be pure by fire but will ruin. But the purity of your faith will bring you praise and glory and honor when Jesus Christ is shown to you. You have not seen Christ, but still you love him. You cannot see him now, but you believe in him. So you are filled with a joy that cannot be explained, a joy full of glory. And you are receiving the goal of your faith—the salvation of your souls.

1 Peter 1:7–9

Loving God means obeying his commands. And God's commands are not too hard for us, because everyone who is a child of God conquers the world. And this is the victory that conquers the world—our faith. So the one who wins against the world is the person who believes that Jesus is the Son of God.

1 John 5:3–5

Then a woman who had been bleeding for twelve years came behind Jesus and touched the edge of his coat. She was thinking, "If I can just touch his clothes, I will be healed." Jesus turned and saw the woman and said, "Be encouraged, dear woman. You are made well because you believed." And the woman was healed from that moment on.

Matthew 9:20–22

After Jesus went inside, the blind men went with him. He asked the men, "Do you believe that I can make you see again?" They answered, "Yes, Lord." Then Jesus touched their eyes and said, "Because you believe I can make you see again, it will happen."

Matthew 9:28–29

Anyone who is sick should call the church's elders. They should pray for and pour oil on the person in the name of the Lord. And the prayer that is said with faith will make the sick person well; the Lord will heal that person. And if the person has sinned, the sins will be forgiven.

James 5:14–15

WHAT THE BIBLE HAS TO SAY
ABOUT

Love

Dear friends, we should love each other, because love comes from God. Everyone who loves has become God's child and knows God. Whoever does not love does not know God, because God is love.

1 John 4:7–8

I may speak in different languages of people or even angels. But if I do not have love, I am only a noisy bell or a crashing cymbal. I may have the gift of prophecy. I may understand all the secret things of God and have all knowledge, and I may have faith so great I can move mountains. But even with all these things, if I do not have love, then I am nothing. I may give away everything I have, and I may even give my body as an offering to be burned. But I gain nothing if I do not have love. Love is patient and kind. Love is not jealous, it does not brag, and it is not proud. Love is not rude, is not selfish, and does not get upset with others. Love does not count up wrongs that have been done. Love is not happy with evil but is happy with the truth. Love patiently accepts all things. It always trusts, always hopes, and always remains strong. Love never ends. There are gifts of prophecy, but they will be ended. There are gifts of speaking in different languages, but those gifts will stop. There is the gift of knowledge, but it will come to an end. So these three things continue forever: faith, hope, and love. And the greatest of these is love.

1 Corinthians 13:1–8, 13

This is what real love is: It is not our love for God; it is God's love for us in sending his Son to be the way to take away our sins. Dear friends, if God loved us that much we also should love each other. No one has ever seen God, but if we love each other, God lives in us, and his love is made perfect in us.

1 John 4:10–12

I loved you as the Father loved me. Now remain in my love. I have obeyed my Father's commands, and I remain in his love. In the same way, if you obey my commands, you will remain in my love.

John 15:9–10

Those who know my commands and obey them are the ones who love me, and my Father will love those who love me. I will love them and will show myself to them.

John 14:21

This is my command: Love each other as I have loved you. The greatest love a person can show is to die for his friends. You are my friends if you do what I command you. This is my command: Love each other.

John 15:12–14, 17

"I give you a new command: Love each other. You must love each other as I have loved you. All people will know that you are my followers if you love each other."

"Love the Lord your God with all your heart, all your soul, all your mind, and all your strength." The second command is this: "Love your neighbor as you love yourself." There are no commands more important than these.

Mark 12:30–31

And so we know the love that God has for us, and we trust that love. God is love. Those who live in love live in God, and God lives in them. We love because God first loved us. If people say, "I love God," but hate their brothers or sisters, they are liars. Those who do not love their brothers and sisters, whom they have seen, cannot love God, whom they have never seen. And God gave us this command: Those who love God must also love their brothers and sisters.

1 John 4:16, 19–21

And from far away the LORD appeared to his people and said, "I love you people with a love that will last forever. That is why I have continued showing you kindness."

Jeremiah 31:3

The Father himself loves you. He loves you because you loved me and believed that I came from God.

John 16:27

But God shows his great love for us in this way: Christ died for us while we were still sinners.

Romans 5:8

God loved the world so much that he gave his one and only Son so that whoever believes in him may not be lost, but have eternal life.

John 3:16

But in all these things we have full victory through God who showed his love for us. Yes, I am sure that neither death, nor life, nor angels, nor ruling spirits, nothing now, nothing in the future, no powers, nothing above us, nothing below us, nor anything else in the whole world will ever be able to separate us from the love of God that is in Christ Jesus our Lord.

Romans 8:37–39

WHAT THE BIBLE HAS TO SAY ABOUT

Eternal Life

This is what God told us: God has given us eternal life, and this life is in his Son. Whoever has the Son has life, but whoever does not have the Son of God does not have life.

1 John 5:11–12

I tell you the truth, whoever hears what I say and believes in the One who sent me has eternal life. That person will not be judged guilty but has already left death and entered life.

John 5:24

God loved the world so much that he gave his one and only Son so that whoever believes in him may not be lost, but have eternal life. God did not send his Son into the world to judge the world guilty, but to save the world through him. People who believe in God's Son are not judged guilty. Those who do not believe have already been judged guilty, because they have not believed in God's one and only Son.

John 3:16–18

No one has seen the Father except the One who is from God; only he has seen the Father. I tell you the truth, whoever believes has eternal life.

John 6:46–47

Here is the bread that comes down from heaven. Anyone who eats this bread will never die. I am the living bread that came down from heaven. Anyone who eats this bread will live forever. This bread is my flesh, which I will give up so that the world may have life.

John 6:50–51

We also know that the Son of God has come and has given us understanding so that we can know the True One. And our lives are in the True One and in his Son, Jesus Christ. He is the true God and the eternal life.

1 John 5:20

Poor people will eat until they are full; those who look to the LORD will praise him. May your hearts live forever!

Psalm 22:26

The LORD watches over the lives of the innocent, and their reward will last forever.

Psalm 37:18

Surely your goodness and love will be with me all my life, and I will live in the house of the LORD forever.

Psalm 23:6

But God will save my life and will take me from the grave.

Psalm 49:15

So this body that can be destroyed will clothe itself with that which can never be destroyed, and this body that dies will clothe itself with that which can never die. When this happens, this Scripture will be made true: "Death is destroyed forever in victory." "Death, where is your victory? Death, where is your pain?" Death's power to hurt is sin, and the power of sin is the law. But we thank God! He gives us the victory through our Lord Jesus Christ.

1 Corinthians 15:54–57

Jesus said to her, "I am the resurrection and the life. Those who believe in me will have life even if they die. And everyone who lives and believes in me will never die."

John 11:25–26

Don't work for the food that spoils. Work for the food that stays good always and gives eternal life. The Son of Man will give you this food, because on him God the Father has put his power.

John 6:27

My sheep listen to my voice; I know them, and they follow me. I give them eternal life, and they will never die, and no one can steal them out of my hand.

John 10:27–28

Jesus answered, "Everyone who drinks this water will be thirsty again, but whoever drinks the water I give will never be thirsty. The water I give will become a spring of water gushing up inside that person, giving eternal life."

John 4:13–14

WHAT THE BIBLE HAS TO SAY ABOUT

Death

We will all die some day. We're like water spilled on the ground; no one can gather it back. But God doesn't take away life. Instead, he plans ways that those who have been sent away will not have to stay away from him!

2 Samuel 14:14

What person alive will not die? Who can escape the grave?

Psalm 89:48

The same thing happens to animals and to people; they both have the same breath, so they both die. . . . Both end up the same way; both came from dust and both will go back to dust.

Ecclesiastes 3:19a–20

No one can control the wind or stop his own death. No soldier is released in times of war, and evil does not set free those who do evil.

Ecclesiastes 8:8

See, even wise people die. Fools and stupid people also die and leave their wealth to others. Even rich people do not live forever; like the animals, people die. But God will save my life and will take me from the grave.

Psalm 49:10, 12, 15

Jesus said, "You people are from here below, but I am from above. You belong to this world, but I don't belong to this world. So I told you that you would die in your sins. Yes, you will die in your sins if you don't believe that I am he."

John 8:23–24

In the past you were spiritually dead because of your sins and the things you did against God.

Ephesians 2:1

When you were baptized, you were buried with Christ, and you were raised up with him through your faith in God's power that was shown when he raised Christ from the dead. When you were spiritually dead because of your sins and because you were not free from the power of your sinful self, God made you alive with Christ, and he forgave all our sins.

Colossians 2:12–13

I tell you the truth, whoever obeys my teaching will never die.

John 8:51

Jesus said to her, "I am the resurrection and the life. Those who believe in me will have life even if they die."

John 11:25

It is now shown to us by the coming of our Savior Christ Jesus. He destroyed death, and through the

Good News he showed us the way to have life that cannot be destroyed.

2 Timothy 1:10

Respect for the Lord gives life. It is like a fountain that can save people from death. The wicked are ruined by their own evil, but those who do right are protected even in death.

Proverbs 14:27, 32

If we live, we are living for the Lord, and if we die, we are dying for the Lord. So living or dying, we belong to the Lord. The reason Christ died and rose from the dead to live again was so he would be Lord over both the dead and the living.

Romans 14:8–9

Just as the Father raises the dead and gives them life, so also the Son gives life to those he wants to. I tell you the truth, whoever hears what I say and believes in the One who sent me has eternal life. That person will not be judged guilty but has already left death and entered life.

John 5:21, 24

WHAT THE BIBLE HAS TO SAY
ABOUT

Praise

The people I made will sing songs to praise me.
Isaiah 43:21

But you are a chosen people, royal priests, a holy nation, a people for God's own possession. You were chosen to tell about the wonderful acts of God, who called you out of darkness into his wonderful light.
1 Peter 2:9

Here on earth we do not have a city that lasts forever, but we are looking for the city that we will have in the future. So through Jesus let us always offer to God our sacrifice of praise, coming from lips that speak his name.
Hebrews 13:14–15

Praise the LORD! It is good to sing praises to our God; it is good and pleasant to praise him.
Psalm 147:1

I will call to the LORD, who is worthy of praise, and I will be saved from my enemies.
2 Samuel 22:4

I will praise the LORD at all times; his praise is always on my lips. My whole being praises the LORD.

The poor will hear and be glad. Glorify the LORD with me, and let us praise his name together.

Psalm 34:1–3

Let them give thanks to the LORD for his love and for the miracles he does for people.

Psalm 107:8

Do not be drunk with wine, which will ruin you, but be filled with the Spirit. Speak to each other with psalms, hymns, and spiritual songs, singing and making music in your hearts to the Lord. Always give thanks to God the Father for everything, in the name of our Lord Jesus Christ.

Ephesians 5:18–20

Clap your hands, all you people. Shout to God with joy. The LORD Most High is wonderful. He is the great King over all the earth! Sing praises to God. Sing praises. Sing praises to our King. Sing praises. God is King of all the earth, so sing a song of praise to him.

Psalm 47:1–2, 6–7

The LORD is great; he should be praised in the city of our God, on his holy mountain.

Psalm 48:1

Those people honor me who bring me offerings to show thanks. And I, God, will save those who do that.

Psalm 50:23

Because your love is better than life, I will praise you. I will praise you as long as I live. I will lift up my hands in prayer to your name. I will be content as if I had eaten the best foods. My lips will sing, and my mouth will praise you.

Psalm 63:3–5

Lord, you are my hope. Lord, I have trusted you since I was young. I have depended on you since I was born; you helped me even on the day of my birth. I will always praise you. I am an example to many people, because you are my strong protection. I am always praising you; all day long I honor you.

Psalm 71:5–8

It is good to praise you, Lord, to sing praises to God Most High. It is good to tell of your love in the morning and of your loyalty at night. Lord, you have made me happy by what you have done; I will sing for joy about what your hands have done. Lord, you have done such great things! How deep are your thoughts!

Psalm 92:1–2, 4–5

The Lord is great; he should be praised at all times. He should be honored more than all the gods, because all the gods of the nations are only idols, but the Lord made the heavens. The Lord has glory and majesty; he has power and beauty in his Temple. Praise the Lord, all nations on earth; praise the Lord's glory and power. Praise the glory of the Lord's name. Bring an offering and come into his Temple courtyards.

Psalm 96:4–8

About midnight Paul and Silas were praying and singing songs to God as the other prisoners listened.

Acts 16:25

WHAT THE BIBLE HAS TO SAY
ABOUT

Serving God

Serve only the LORD your God. Respect him, keep his commands, and obey him. Serve him and be loyal to him.

Deuteronomy 13:4

No one can serve two masters. The person will hate one master and love the other, or will follow one master and refuse to follow the other. You cannot serve both God and worldly riches.

Matthew 6:24

Jesus said to the devil, "Go away from me, Satan! It is written in the Scriptures, 'You must worship the Lord your God and serve only him.'" So the devil left Jesus, and angels came and took care of him.

Matthew 4:10–11

But be careful to obey the teachings and laws Moses, the LORD's servant, gave you: to love the LORD your God and obey his commands, to continue to follow him and serve him the very best you can.

Joshua 22:5

So brothers and sisters, since God has shown us great mercy, I beg you to offer your lives as a living sacrifice to him. Your offering must be only for God and pleasing to him, which is the spiritual way for you to worship. Do not change yourselves to be like the people of this world, but be changed within by a new way of thinking. Then you will be able to decide what God wants for you; you will know what is good and pleasing to him and what is perfect.

Romans 12:1–2

Love each other like brothers and sisters. Give each other more honor than you want for yourselves. Do not be lazy but work hard, serving the Lord with all your heart. Share with God's people who need help. Bring strangers in need into your homes.

Romans 12:10–11, 13

Shout to the Lord, all the earth. Serve the Lord with joy; come before him with singing.

Psalm 100:1–2

If you worship the Lord your God, I will bless your bread and your water. I will take away sickness from you.

Exodus 23:25

Now, Israel, this is what the Lord your God wants you to do: Respect the Lord your God, and do what he has told you to do. Love him. Serve the Lord your God with your whole being, and obey the Lord's commands and laws that I am giving you today for your own good.

Deuteronomy 10:12–13

If you carefully obey the commands I am giving

you today and love the LORD your God and serve him with your whole being, then he will send rain on your land at the right time, in the fall and spring, and you will be able to gather your grain, new wine, and oil. He will put grass in the fields for your cattle, and you will have plenty to eat.

Deuteronomy 11:13–15

But if you don't want to serve the LORD, you must choose for yourselves today whom you will serve. You may serve the gods that your ancestors worshiped when they lived on the other side of the Euphrates River, or you may serve the gods of the Amorites who lived in this land. As for me and my family, we will serve the LORD.

Joshua 24:15

Samuel answered, "Don't be afraid. It's true that you did wrong, but don't turn away from the LORD. Serve the LORD with all your heart. Idols are of no use, so don't worship them. They can't help you or save you. They are useless! For his own sake, the LORD won't leave his people. Instead, he was pleased to make you his own people."

1 Samuel 12:20–22

Young people, enjoy yourselves while you are young; be happy while you are young. Do whatever your heart desires, whatever you want to do. But remember that God will judge you for everything you do.

Ecclesiastes 11:9

And you, my son Solomon, accept the God of your father. Serve him completely and willingly, because the LORD knows what is in everyone's mind. He understands everything you think. If you go to him for help, you will get an answer. But if you turn away from him, he will leave you forever.

1 Chronicles 28:9

In the past, the law held us like prisoners, but our old selves died, and we were made free from the law. So now we serve God in a new way with the Spirit, and not in the old way with written rules.

Romans 7:6

WHAT THE BIBLE HAS TO SAY ABOUT

Being Obedient

See, today I am letting you choose a blessing or a curse. You will be blessed if you obey the commands of the LORD your God that I am giving you today. But you will be cursed if you disobey the commands of the LORD your God. So do not disobey the commands I am giving you today, and do not worship other gods you do not know.

Deuteronomy 11:26–28

But Samuel answered, "What pleases the LORD more: burnt offerings and sacrifices or obedience to his voice? It is better to obey than to sacrifice. It is better to listen to God than to offer the fat of sheep."

1 Samuel 15:22

This is what the LORD, who saves you, the Holy One of Israel, says: "I am the LORD your God, who teaches you to do what is good, who leads you in the way you should go. If you had obeyed me, you would have had peace like a full-flowing river. Good things would have flowed to you like the waves of the sea."

Isaiah 48:17–18

I also gave them this command: Obey me, and I will be your God and you will be my people. Do all that I command so that good things will happen to you.

Jeremiah 7:23

If you love me, you will obey my commands. Those who know my commands and obey them are the ones who love me, and my Father will love those who love me. I will love them and will show myself to them.

John 14:15, 21

Peter and the other apostles answered, "We must obey God, not human authority!"

Acts 5:29

He is the way our sins are taken away, and not only our sins but the sins of all people. We can be sure that we know God if we obey his commands. Anyone who says, "I know God," but does not obey God's commands is a liar, and the truth is not in that person. But if someone obeys God's teaching, then in that person God's love has truly reached its goal. This is how we can be sure we are living in God: Whoever says that he lives in God must live as Jesus lived.

1 John 2:2–6

If you follow me and obey my laws and commands, as your father David did, I will also give you a long life.

1 Kings 3:14

Teach me to do what you want, because you are my God. Let your good Spirit lead me on level ground.

Psalm 143:10

Moses called all the people of Israel together and said: Listen, Israel, to the commands and laws I am giving you today. Learn them and obey them carefully. So be careful to do what the LORD your God has commanded you, and follow the commands exactly. Live the way the LORD your God has commanded you so that you may live and have what is good and have a long life in the land you will take.

Deuteronomy 5:1, 32–33

For the Lord's sake, yield to the people who have authority in this world: the king, who is the highest authority, and the leaders who are sent by him to punish those who do wrong and to praise those who do right. It is God's desire that by doing good you should stop foolish people from saying stupid things about you. Live as free people, but do not use your freedom as an excuse to do evil. Live as servants of God. Show respect for all people: Love the brothers and sisters of God's family, respect God, honor the king. Slaves, yield to the authority of your masters with all respect, not only those who are good and kind, but also those who are dishonest. A person might have to suffer even when it is unfair, but if he thinks of God and stands the pain, God is pleased. If you are beaten for doing wrong, there is no reason to praise you for being patient in your punishment. But if you suffer for doing good, and you are patient, then God is pleased. This is what you were called to do, because Christ suffered for you and gave you an example to follow. So you should do as he did.

1 Peter 2:13–21

Children, obey your parents as the Lord wants, because this is the right thing to do. The command says, "Honor your father and mother." This is the first command that has a promise with it.—"Then everything will be well with you, and you will have a long life on the earth."

Ephesians 6:1–3

Children, obey your parents in all things, because this pleases the Lord. Slaves, obey your masters in all things. Do not obey just when they are watching you, to gain their favor, but serve them honestly, because you respect the Lord. In all the work you are doing, work the best you can. Work as if you were doing it for the Lord, not for people. Remember that you will receive your reward from the Lord, which he promised to his people. You are serving the Lord Christ.

Colossians 3:20, 22–24

WHAT THE BIBLE HAS TO SAY ABOUT

The Worldly Mind

If people's thinking is controlled by the sinful self, there is death. But if their thinking is controlled by the Spirit, there is life and peace. When people's thinking is controlled by the sinful self, they are against God, because they refuse to obey God's law and really are not even able to obey God's law. Those people who are ruled by their sinful selves cannot please God.

Romans 8:6-8

If they plant to satisfy their sinful selves, their sinful selves will bring them ruin. But if they plant to please the Spirit, they will receive eternal life from the Spirit. We must not become tired of doing good. We will receive our harvest of eternal life at the right time if we do not give up.

Galatians 6:8-9

You want things, but you do not have them. So you are ready to kill and are jealous of other people, but you still cannot get what you want. So you argue and fight. You do not get what you want, because you do not ask God. Or when you ask, you do not receive because the reason you ask is wrong. You want things so you can use them for your own pleasures. So, you are not loyal to God! You should know that loving the world is the same as hating God. Anyone who wants to be a friend of the world becomes God's enemy.

James 4:2–4

Some people think they are doing right, but in the end it leads to death. Someone who is laughing may be sad inside, and joy may end in sadness. Evil people will be paid back for their evil ways, and good people will be rewarded for their good ones.

Proverbs 14:12–14

Many people live like enemies of the cross of Christ. I have often told you about them, and it makes me cry to tell you about them now. In the end, they will be destroyed. They do whatever their bodies want, they are proud of their shameful acts, and they think only about earthly things. But our homeland is in heaven, and we are waiting for our Savior, the Lord Jesus Christ, to come from heaven. By his power to rule all things, he will change our simple bodies and make them like his own glorious body.

Philippians 3:18–21

Share in the troubles we have like a good soldier of Christ Jesus. A soldier wants to please the enlisting officer, so no one serving in the army wastes time with everyday matters. Also an athlete who takes part in a contest must obey all the rules in order to win. But run away from the evil young people like to do. Try hard to live right and to have faith, love, and peace, together with those who trust in the Lord from pure hearts. Stay away from foolish and stupid arguments, because you know they grow into quarrels.

2 Timothy 2:3–5, 22–23

Remember this! In the last days there will be many troubles, because people will love themselves, love money, brag, and be proud. They will say evil things against others and will not obey their parents or be thankful or be the kind of people God wants. They will not love others, will refuse to forgive, will gossip, and will not control themselves. They will be cruel, will hate what is good, will turn against their friends, and will do foolish things without thinking. They will be conceited, will love pleasure instead of God, and will act as if they serve God but will not have his power. Stay away from those people. Some of them go into homes and get control of silly women who are full of sin and are led by many evil desires. These women are always learning new teachings, but they are never able to understand the truth fully.

2 Timothy 3:1–7

Dear friends, you are like foreigners and strangers in this world. I beg you to avoid the evil things your bodies want to do that fight against your soul. People who do not believe are living all around you and might say that you are doing wrong. Live such good lives that they will see the good things you do and will give glory to God on the day when Christ comes again.

1 Peter 2:11–12

Do not love the world or the things in the world. If you love the world, the love of the Father is not in you. These are the ways of the world: wanting to please our sinful selves, wanting the sinful things we see, and being too proud of what we have. None of these come from the Father, but all of them come from the world. The world and everything that people want in it are passing away, but the person who does what God wants lives forever.

1 John 2:15–17

So brothers and sisters, since God has shown us great mercy, I beg you to offer your lives as a living sacrifice to him. Your offering must be only for God and pleasing to him, which is the spiritual way for you to worship. Do not change yourselves to be like the people of this world, but be changed within by a new way of thinking. Then you will be able to decide what God wants for you; you will know what is good and pleasing to him and what is perfect. Your love must be real. Hate what is evil, and hold on to what is good.

Romans 12:1–2, 9

When you do things, do not let selfishness or pride be your guide. Instead, be humble and give more honor to others than to yourselves. Do not be interested only in your own life, but be interested in the lives of others. In your lives you must think and act like Christ Jesus.

Philippians 2:3–5

You, Lord, give true peace to those who depend on you, because they trust you. So, trust the Lord always, because he is our Rock forever.

Isaiah 26:3–4

Think only about the things in heaven, not the things on earth. So put all evil things out of your life: sexual sinning, doing evil, letting evil thoughts control you, wanting things that are evil, and greed. This is really serving a false god. These things make God angry. But now also put these things out of your life: anger, bad temper, doing or saying things to hurt others, and using evil words when you talk. Do not lie to each other. You have left your old sinful life and the things you did before. You have begun to live the new life, in which you are being made new and are becoming like the One who made you. This new life brings you the true knowledge of God.

Colossians 3:2, 5–6, 8–10

Brothers and sisters, think about the things that are good and worthy of praise. Think about the things that are true and honorable and right and pure and beautiful and respected.

Philippians 4:8

Unacceptable Sexual Behavior

God's anger is shown from heaven against all the evil and wrong things people do. By their own evil lives they hide the truth. They knew God, but they did not give glory to God or thank him. Their thinking became useless. Their foolish minds were filled with darkness. Because people did those things, God left them and let them do the shameful things they wanted to do. Women stopped having natural sex and started having sex with other women. In the same way, men stopped having natural sex and began wanting each other. Men did shameful things with other men, and in their bodies they received the punishment for those wrongs. People did not think it was important to have a true knowledge of God. So God left them and allowed them to have their own worthless thinking and to do things they should not do.

Romans 1:18, 21, 26–28

We also know that the law is not made for good people but for those who are against the law and for those who refuse to follow it. It is for people who are against God and are sinful, who are not holy and have no religion, who kill their fathers and mothers, who murder, who take part in sexual sins, who have sexual relations with people of the same sex, who sell slaves, who tell lies, who speak falsely, and who do anything against the true teaching of God. That teaching is part of the Good News of the blessed God that he gave me to tell.

1 Timothy 1:9–11

My son, don't be held captive by a woman who takes part in adultery. . . .

Proverbs 5:20a

Surely you know that the people who do wrong will not inherit God's kingdom. Do not be fooled. Those who sin sexually, worship idols, take part in adultery, those who are male prostitutes, or men who have sexual relations with other men, those who steal, are greedy, get drunk, lie about others, or rob—these people will not inherit God's kingdom. In the past, some of you were like that, but you were washed clean. You were made holy, and you were made right with God in the name of the Lord Jesus Christ and in the Spirit of our God.

1 Corinthians 6:9–11

Brothers and sisters, we taught you how to live in a way that will please God, and you are living that way. Now we ask and encourage you in the Lord Jesus to live that way even more. You know what we told you to do by the authority of the Lord Jesus. God wants you to be holy and to stay away from sexual sins. He wants each of you to learn to control your own body in a way that is holy and honorable. Don't use your body for sexual sin like the people who do not know God.

1 Thessalonians 4:1–5

My son, keep your father's commands, and don't forget your mother's teaching. Keep their words in mind forever as though you had them tied around your neck. They will guide you when you walk. They will guard you when you sleep. They will speak to you when you are awake. These commands are like a lamp; this teaching is like a light. And the correction that comes from them will help you have life. They will keep you from sinful women and from the pleasing words of another man's unfaithful wife. Don't desire her because she is beautiful. Don't let her capture you by the way she looks at you. A prostitute will treat you like a loaf of bread, and a woman who takes part in adultery may cost you your life. You cannot carry hot coals against your chest without burning your clothes, and you cannot walk on hot coals without burning your feet. The same is true if you have sexual relations with another man's wife. Anyone who does so will be punished.

Proverbs 6:20–29

"I am allowed to do all things," but all things are not good for me to do. "I am allowed to do all things," but I will not let anything make me its slave. "Food is for the stomach, and the stomach for food," but God will destroy them both. The body is not for sexual sin but for the Lord, and the Lord is for the body.

1 Corinthians 6:12–13

You must not be guilty of adultery.

Exodus 20:14

So run away from sexual sin. Every other sin people do is outside their bodies, but those who sin sexually sin against their own bodies. You should know that your body is a temple for the Holy Spirit who is in you. You have received the Holy Spirit from God. So you do not belong to yourselves.

1 Corinthians 6:18–19

More than anything else, a person's mind is evil and cannot be healed. No one truly understands it. But I, the LORD, look into a person's heart and test the mind. So I can decide what each one deserves; I can give each one the right payment for what he does.

Jeremiah 17:9–10

But if we confess our sins, he will forgive our sins, because we can trust God to do what is right. He will cleanse us from all the wrongs we have done.

1 John 1:9

He is the way our sins are taken away, and not only our sins but the sins of all people.

1 John 2:2

You must not have sexual relations with a man as

you would a woman. That is a hateful sin. You must not have sexual relations with an animal and make yourself unclean with it. Also a woman must not have sexual relations with an animal; it is not natural. Don't make yourself unclean by any of these wrong things. . . .

Leviticus 18:22–24a

You have heard that it was said, "You must not be guilty of adultery." But I tell you that if anyone looks at a woman and wants to sin sexually with her, in his mind he has already done that sin with the woman.

Matthew 5:27, 28

If a man has sexual relations with another man as a man does with a woman, these two men have done a hateful sin. They must be put to death. They have brought it on themselves.

Leviticus 20:13

Enjoy serving the LORD, and he will give you what you want. Depend on the LORD; trust him, and he will take care of you.

Psalm 37:4–5

God, your love is so precious! You protect people in the shadow of your wings.

Psalm 36:7

Be faithful to your own wife, just as you drink water from your own well.

Proverbs 5:15

Those who go to God Most High for safety will be protected by the Almighty. I will say to the LORD, "You are my place of safety and protection. You are my God and I trust you." God will save you from hidden traps and from deadly diseases.

Psalm 91:1–3

WHAT THE BIBLE HAS TO SAY ABOUT

Substance Abuse

You should know that your body is a temple for the Holy Spirit who is in you. You have received the Holy Spirit from God. So you do not belong to yourselves, because you were bought by God for a price. So honor God with your bodies.

1 Corinthians 6:19–20

Do not be drunk with wine, which will ruin you, but be filled with the Spirit.

Ephesians 5:18

A thief comes to steal and kill and destroy, but I came to give life—life in all its fullness.

John 10:10

Anyone who is having troubles should pray. Anyone who is happy should sing praises.

James 5:13

Two people are better than one, because they get more done by working together. If one falls down, the other can help him up. But it is bad for the person who is alone and falls, because no one is there to help.

Ecclesiastes 4:9–10

If we say we have no sin, we are fooling ourselves, and the truth is not in us. But if we confess our sins, he will forgive our sins, because we can trust God to do what is right. He will cleanse us from all the wrongs we have done.

1 John 1:8–9

All of you must yield to the government rulers. No one rules unless God has given him the power to rule, and no one rules now without that power from God. So those who are against the government are really against what God has commanded. And they will bring punishment on themselves. Those who do right do not have to fear the rulers; only those who do wrong fear them. Do you want to be unafraid of the rulers? Then do what is right, and they will praise you. The ruler is God's servant to help you. But if you do wrong, then be afraid. He has the power to punish; he is God's servant to punish those who do wrong. So you must yield to the government, not only because you might be punished, but because you know it is right.

Romans 13:1–5

The "night" is almost finished, and the "day" is almost here. So we should stop doing things that belong to darkness and take up the weapons used for fighting in the light. Let us live in a right way, like people who belong to the day. We should not have wild parties or get drunk. There should be no sexual sins of any kind, no fighting or jealousy. But clothe yourselves with the Lord Jesus Christ and forget about satisfying your sinful self.

Romans 13:12–14

Listen, my child, and be wise. Keep your mind on what is right. Don't drink too much wine or eat too much food. Those who drink and eat too much become poor. They sleep too much and end up wearing rags. Learn the truth and never reject it. Get wisdom, self-control, and understanding.

Proverbs 23:19–21, 23

Give all your worries to him, because he cares about you. Control yourselves and be careful! The devil, your enemy, goes around like a roaring lion looking for someone to eat.

1 Peter 5:7–8

Praise be to the God and Father of our Lord Jesus Christ. God is the Father who is full of mercy and all comfort. He comforts us every time we have trouble, so when others have trouble, we can comfort them with the same comfort God gives us.

2 Corinthians 1:3–4

The Grace of God

With great power the apostles were telling people that the Lord Jesus was truly raised from the dead. And God blessed all the believers very much.

Acts 4:33

Don't ever forget kindness and truth. Wear them like a necklace. Write them on your heart as if on a tablet. Then you will be respected and will please both God and people. Trust the LORD with all your heart, and don't depend on your own understanding. Remember the LORD in all you do, and he will give you success.

Proverbs 3:3–6

The LORD God is like a sun and shield; the LORD gives us kindness and honor. He does not hold back anything good from those whose lives are innocent.

Psalm 84:11

Then the LORD said to Moses, "I will do what you ask, because I know you very well, and I am pleased with you." Then Moses said, "Now, please show me your glory." The LORD answered, "I will cause all my goodness to pass in front of you, and I will announce my name, the LORD, so you can hear it. I will show kindness to anyone to whom I want to show kindness, and I will show mercy to anyone to whom I want to show mercy."

Exodus 33:17–19

You gave me life and showed me kindness, and in your care you watched over my life.

Job 10:12

LORD, you bless those who do what is right; you protect them like a soldier's shield.

Psalm 5:12

Because of his love, God had already decided to make us his own children through Jesus Christ. That was what he wanted and what pleased him, and it brings praise to God because of his wonderful grace. God gave that grace to us freely, in Christ, the One he loves. In Christ we are set free by the blood of his death, and so we have forgiveness of sins. How rich is God's grace,

Ephesians 1:5–7

LORD, in your kindness you made my mountain safe. But when you turned away, I was frightened. I called to you, LORD, and asked you to have mercy on me.

Psalm 30:7–8

The LORD remembers us and will bless us. He will bless the family of Israel; he will bless the family of Aaron. The LORD will bless those who respect him, from the smallest to the greatest.

Psalm 115:12–13

Those who find me find life, and the LORD will be pleased with them.

Proverbs 8:35

Good people will have rich blessings, but the wicked will be overwhelmed by violence. The LORD's blessing brings wealth, and no sorrow comes with it. Evil people will get what they fear most, but good people will get what they want most.

Proverbs 10:6, 22, 24

Stay away from fools, because they can't teach you anything. A wise person will understand what to do, but a foolish person is dishonest. Fools don't care if they sin, but honest people work at being right.

Proverbs 14:7–9

All these things are for you. And so the grace of God that is being given to more and more people will bring increasing thanks to God for his glory.

2 Corinthians 4:15

Let us, then, feel very sure that we can come before God's throne where there is grace. There we can receive mercy and grace to help us when we need it.

Hebrews 4:16

The Holy Spirit

You should know that your body is a temple for the Holy Spirit who is in you. You have received the Holy Spirit from God. So you do not belong to yourselves.

1 Corinthians 6:19

And this hope will never disappoint us, because God has poured out his love to fill our hearts. He gave us his love through the Holy Spirit, whom God has given to us.

Romans 5:5

I will ask the Father, and he will give you another Helper to be with you forever—the Spirit of truth. The world cannot accept him, because it does not see him or know him. But you know him, because he lives with you and he will be in you. I will not leave you all alone like orphans; I will come back to you. In a little while the world will not see me anymore, but you will see me. Because I live, you will live, too. On that day you will know that I am in my Father, and that you are in me and I am in you.

John 14:16–20

But I tell you the truth, it is better for you that I go away. When I go away, I will send the Helper to you. If I do not go away, the Helper will not come. When the Helper comes, he will prove to the people of the world the truth about sin, about being right with God, and about judgment. He will prove to them that sin is not believing in me. The Spirit of truth will bring glory to me, because he will take what I have to say and tell it to you.

John 16:7–9, 14

I baptize you with water to show that your hearts and lives have changed. But there is one coming after me who is greater than I am, whose sandals I am not good enough to carry. He will baptize you with the Holy Spirit and fire.

Matthew 3:11

"If anyone believes in me, rivers of living water will flow out from that person's heart, as the Scripture says." Jesus was talking about the Holy Spirit. The Spirit had not yet been given, because Jesus had not yet been raised to glory. But later, those who believed in Jesus would receive the Spirit.

John 7:38–39

While Apollos was in Corinth, Paul was visiting some places on the way to Ephesus. There he found some followers and asked them, "Did you receive the Holy Spirit when you believed?" They said, "We have never even heard of a Holy Spirit." So he asked, "What kind of baptism did you have?" They said, "It was the baptism that John taught." Paul said, "John's baptism was a baptism of changed hearts and lives.

He told people to believe in the one who would come after him, and that one is Jesus." When they heard this, they were baptized in the name of the Lord Jesus. Then Paul laid his hands on them, and the Holy Spirit came upon them. They began speaking different languages and prophesying.

Acts 19:1–6

So I tell you: Live by following the Spirit. Then you will not do what your sinful selves want. Our sinful selves want what is against the Spirit, and the Spirit wants what is against our sinful selves. The two are against each other, so you cannot do just what you please.

Galatians 5:16–17

Once when he was eating with them, he told them not to leave Jerusalem. He said, "Wait here to receive the promise from the Father which I told you about. John baptized people with water, but in a few days you will be baptized with the Holy Spirit." Jesus said to them, "The Father is the only One who has the authority to decide dates and times. These things are not for you to know. But when the Holy Spirit comes to you, you will receive power. You will be my witnesses—in Jerusalem, in all of Judea, in Samaria, and in every part of the world."

Acts 1:4–5, 7–8

They were all filled with the Holy Spirit, and they began to speak different languages by the power the

Holy Spirit was giving them.

Acts 2:4

Peter said to them, "Change your hearts and lives and be baptized, each one of you, in the name of Jesus Christ for the forgiveness of your sins. And you will receive the gift of the Holy Spirit."

Acts 2:38

After they had prayed, the place where they were meeting was shaken. They were all filled with the Holy Spirit, and they spoke God's word without fear.

Acts 4:31

Do not be drunk with wine, which will ruin you, but be filled with the Spirit. Speak to each other with psalms, hymns, and spiritual songs, singing and making music in your hearts to the Lord. Always give thanks to God the Father for everything, in the name of our Lord Jesus Christ.

Ephesians 5:18–20

When the apostles who were still in Jerusalem heard that the people of Samaria had accepted the word of God, they sent Peter and John to them. When Peter and John arrived, they prayed that the Samaritan believers might receive the Holy Spirit. These people had been baptized in the name of the Lord Jesus, but the Holy Spirit had not yet come upon any of them. Then, when the two apostles began laying their hands on the people, they received the Holy Spirit.

Acts 8:14–17

While Peter was still saying this, the Holy Spirit came down on all those who were listening. The Jewish believers who came with Peter were amazed that the gift of the Holy Spirit had been given even to those who were not Jews. These Jewish believers heard them speaking in different languages and praising God. Then Peter said, "Can anyone keep these people from being baptized with water? They have received the Holy Spirit just as we did!"

Acts 10:44–47

WHAT THE BIBLE HAS TO SAY
ABOUT

God's Faithfulness

LORD, your love fills the earth. Teach me your demands. You have done good things for your servant, as you have promised, LORD.

Psalm 119:64–65

Now may God himself, the God of peace, make you pure, belonging only to him. May your whole self—spirit, soul, and body—be kept safe and without fault when our Lord Jesus Christ comes. You can trust the One who calls you to do that for you.

1 Thessalonians 5:23–24

The LORD says, "This day is like the time of Noah to me. I promised then that I would never flood the world again. In the same way, I promise I will not be angry with you or punish you again. The mountains may disappear, and the hills may come to an end, but my love will never disappear; my promise of peace will not come to an end," says the LORD who shows mercy to you.

Isaiah 54:9–10

"When the rainbow appears in the clouds, I will see it and I will remember the agreement that continues forever between me and every living thing on the earth." So God said to Noah, "The rainbow is a sign of the agreement that I made with all living things on earth."

Genesis 9:16–17

I am with you and will protect you everywhere you go and will bring you back to this land. I will not leave you until I have done what I have promised you.

Genesis 28:15

God, who has called you to share everything with his Son, Jesus Christ our Lord, is faithful.

1 Corinthians 1:9

The only temptation that has come to you is that which everyone has. But you can trust God, who will not permit you to be tempted more than you can stand. But when you are tempted, he will also give you a way to escape so that you will be able to stand it.

1 Corinthians 10:13

If we are not faithful, he will still be faithful, because he cannot be false to himself. But God's strong foundation continues to stand. These words are written on the seal: "The Lord knows those who belong to him," and "Everyone who wants to belong to the Lord must stop doing wrong."

2 Timothy 2:13, 19

But the LORD chose you because he loved you, and he kept his promise to your ancestors. So he brought you out of Egypt by his great power and freed you from the land of slavery, from the power of the king of Egypt. So know that the LORD your God is God, the faithful God. He will keep his agreement of love for a thousand lifetimes for people who love him and obey his commands.

Deuteronomy 7:8–9

It's almost time for me to die. You know and fully believe that the LORD has done great things for you. You know that he has not failed to keep any of his promises.

Joshua 23:14

Praise the LORD! He promised he would give rest to his people Israel, and he has given us rest. The LORD has kept all the good promises he gave through his servant Moses. May the LORD our God be with us as he was with our ancestors. May he never leave us, and may he turn us to himself so we will follow him. Let us obey all the laws and commands he gave our ancestors.

1 Kings 8:56–58

LORD, your love reaches to the heavens, your loyalty to the skies.

Psalm 36:5

I will always sing about the LORD's love; I will tell of his loyalty from now on. I will say, "Your love continues forever; your loyalty goes on and on like the sky." Once, in a vision, you spoke to those who worship you. You said, "I have given strength to a warrior; I have raised up a young man from my people. I will not break my agreement nor change what I have said."

Psalm 89:1–2, 19, 34

He will not let you be defeated. He who guards you never sleeps. The Lord will protect you from all dangers; he will guard your life. The Lord will guard you as you come and go, both now and forever.

Psalm 121:3, 7–8

The Lord is not slow in doing what he promised— the way some people understand slowness. But God is being patient with you. He does not want anyone to be lost, but he wants all people to change their hearts and lives.

2 Peter 3:9

WHAT THE BIBLE HAS TO SAY ABOUT

The Church

His goal was to carry out his plan, when the right time came, that all things in heaven and on earth would be joined together in Christ as the head. God put everything under his power and made him the head over everything for the church, which is Christ's body. The church is filled with Christ, and Christ fills everything in every way.

Ephesians 1:10, 22–23

God has freed us from the power of darkness, and he brought us into the kingdom of his dear Son. He is the head of the body, which is the church. Everything comes from him. He is the first one who was raised from the dead. So in all things Jesus has first place.

Colossians 1:13, 18

Then Jesus asked them, "And who do you say I am?" Simon Peter answered, "You are the Christ, the Son of the living God." Jesus answered, "You are blessed, Simon son of Jonah, because no person taught you that. My Father in heaven showed you who I am. So I tell you, you are Peter. On this rock I will build my church, and the power of death will not be able to defeat it."

Matthew 16:15–18

You are like a building that was built on the foundation of the apostles and prophets. Christ Jesus himself is the most important stone in that building, and that whole building is joined together in Christ. He makes it grow and become a holy temple in the Lord. And in Christ you, too, are being built together with the Jews into a place where God lives through the Spirit.

Ephesians 2:20–22

With God's power working in us, God can do much, much more than anything we can ask or imagine. To him be glory in the church and in Christ Jesus for all time, forever and ever. Amen.

Ephesians 3:20–21

Remember your leaders who taught God's message to you. Remember how they lived and died, and copy their faith. Jesus Christ is the same yesterday, today, and forever. Obey your leaders and act under their authority. They are watching over you, because they are responsible for your souls. Obey them so that they will do this work with joy, not sadness. It will not help you to make their work hard.

Hebrews 13:7–8, 17

They spent their time learning the apostles' teaching, sharing, breaking bread, and praying together. The apostles were doing many miracles and signs, and everyone felt great respect for God. All the believers were together and shared everything. They would sell their land and the things they owned and then divide the money and give it to anyone who needed it. The believers met together in the Temple every day. They ate together in their homes, happy to share their food with joyful hearts. They praised God and were liked by all the people. Every day the Lord added those who were being saved to the group of believers.

Acts 2:42–47

No one ever hates his own body, but feeds and takes care of it. And that is what Christ does for the church, because we are parts of his body.

Ephesians 5:29–30

Be sure that no one leads you away with false and empty teaching that is only human, which comes from the ruling spirits of this world, and not from Christ. All of God lives in Christ fully (even when Christ was on earth), and you have a full and true life in Christ, who is ruler over all rulers and powers.

Colossians 2:8–10

Each one of us has a body with many parts, and these parts all have different uses. In the same way, we are many, but in Christ we are all one body. Each one is a part of that body, and each part belongs to all the other parts. We all have different gifts, each of which came because of the grace God gave us. The person who has the gift of prophecy should use that gift in agreement with the faith. Anyone who has the gift of serving should serve. Anyone who has the gift of teaching should teach. Whoever has the gift of encouraging others should encourage. Whoever has the gift of giving to others should give freely. Anyone who has the gift of being a leader should try hard when he leads. Whoever has the gift of showing mercy to others should do so with joy.

Romans 12:4–8

A person's body is only one thing, but it has many parts. Though there are many parts to a body, all those parts make only one body. Christ is like that also. Some of us are Jews, and some are Greeks. Some of us are slaves, and some are free. But we were all baptized into one body through one Spirit. And we were all made to share in the one Spirit. The human body has many parts. The foot might say, "Because I am not a hand, I am not part of the body." But saying this would not stop the foot from being a part of the body. The ear might say, "Because I am not an eye, I am not part of the body." But saying this would not stop the ear from being a part of the body. If the whole body were an eye, it would not be able to hear. If the whole body were an ear, it would not be able to smell. If each part of the body were the same part, there would be no body. But truly God put all the parts, each one of them, in the body as he wanted them. So then there are many parts, but only one body. The eye cannot say to the hand, "I don't need you!" And the head cannot say to the foot, "I don't need you!"

No! Those parts of the body that seem to be the weaker are really necessary. And the parts of the body we think are less are the parts to which we give the most honor. We give special respect to the parts we want to hide. The more respectable parts of our body need no special care. But God put the body together and gave more honor to the parts that need it so our body would not be divided. God wanted the different parts to care the same for each other. If one part of the body suffers, all the other parts suffer with it. Or if one part of our body is honored, all the other parts share its honor. Together you are the body of Christ, and each one of you is a part of that body. In the church God has given a place first to apostles, second to prophets, and third to teachers. Then God has given a place to those who do miracles, those who have gifts of healing, those who can help others, those who are able to govern, and those who can speak in different languages.

1 Corinthians 12:12–28

Now, brothers and sisters, we ask you to appreciate those who work hard among you, who lead you in the Lord and teach you. Respect them with a very special love because of the work they do. Live in peace with each other.

1 Thessalonians 5:12–13

And Christ gave gifts to people—he made some to be apostles, some to be prophets, some to go and tell the Good News, and some to have the work of caring for and teaching God's people. Christ gave those gifts to prepare God's holy people for the work of serving, to make the body of Christ stronger. This work must continue until we are all joined together in the same faith and in the same knowledge of the Son of God. We must become like a mature person, growing until we become like Christ and have his perfection.

Ephesians 4:11–13

It is good and pleasant when God's people live together in peace!

Psalm 133:1

WHAT THE BIBLE HAS TO SAY ABOUT

Discipleship

Then Jesus came to them and said, "All power in heaven and on earth is given to me. So go and make followers of all people in the world. Baptize them in the name of the Father and the Son and the Holy Spirit. Teach them to obey everything that I have taught you, and I will be with you always, even until the end of this age."

Matthew 28:18–20

A student is not better than the teacher, but the student who has been fully trained will be like the teacher.

Luke 6:40

Then Barnabas went to the city of Tarsus to look for Saul, and when he found Saul, he brought him to Antioch. For a whole year Saul and Barnabas met with the church and taught many people there. In Antioch the followers were called Christians for the first time.

Acts 11:25–26

Jesus said to all of them, "If people want to follow me, they must give up the things they want. They must be willing to give up their lives daily to follow me. Those who want to save their lives will give up true life. But those who give up their lives for me will have true life. It is worth nothing for them to have the whole world if they themselves are destroyed or lost. If people are ashamed of me and my teaching, then the Son of Man will be ashamed of them when he comes in his glory and with the glory of the Father and the holy angels."

Luke 9:23–26

If anyone comes to me but loves his father, mother, wife, children, brothers, or sisters—or even life—more than me, he cannot be my follower.

Luke 14:26

Let us think about each other and help each other to show love and do good deeds. You should not stay away from the church meetings, as some are doing, but you should meet together and encourage each other. Do this even more as you see the day coming.

Hebrews 10:24–25

As they were going along the road, someone said to Jesus, "I will follow you any place you go." Jesus said to them, "The foxes have holes to live in, and the birds have nests, but the Son of Man has no place to rest his head." Jesus said to another man, "Follow me!" But he said, "Lord, first let me go and bury my father." But Jesus said to him, "Let the people who are dead bury their own dead. You must go and tell about the kingdom of God." Another man said, "I will follow you, Lord, but first let me go and say good-bye to my family." Jesus said, "Anyone who begins to plow a field but keeps looking back is of no use in the kingdom of God."

Luke 9:57–62

I can do all things through Christ, because he gives me strength.

Philippians 4:13

Whoever serves me must follow me. Then my servant will be with me everywhere I am. My Father will honor anyone who serves me.

John 12:26

After this, Jesus went out and saw a tax collector named Levi sitting in the tax collector's booth. Jesus said to him, "Follow me!" So Levi got up, left everything, and followed him.

Luke 5:27–28

I think that all things are worth nothing compared with the greatness of knowing Christ Jesus my Lord. Because of him, I have lost all those things, and now I know they are worthless trash. This allows me to have Christ and to belong to him. Now I am right with God, not because I followed the law, but because I believed in Christ. God uses my faith to make me right with him.

Philippians 3:8–9

You should teach people whom you can trust the things you and many others have heard me say. Then they will be able to teach others.

2 Timothy 2:2

WHAT THE BIBLE HAS TO SAY ABOUT

Stewardship

"Should a person rob God? But you are robbing me. You ask, 'How have we robbed you?' You have robbed me in your offerings and the tenth of your crops. So a curse is on you, because the whole nation has robbed me. Bring to the storehouse a full tenth of what you earn so there will be food in my house. Test me in this," says the LORD All-Powerful. "I will open the windows of heaven for you and pour out all the blessings you need. I will stop the insects so they won't eat your crops. The grapes won't fall from your vines before they are ready to pick," says the LORD All-Powerful. "All the nations will call you blessed, because you will have a pleasant country," says the LORD All-Powerful.

Malachi 3:8–12

Now I will write about the collection of money for God's people. Do the same thing I told the Galatian churches to do: On the first day of every week, each one of you should put aside money as you have been blessed.

1 Corinthians 16:1–2a

Remember this: The person who plants a little will have a small harvest, but the person who plants a lot will have a big harvest. Each one should give as you have decided in your heart to give. You should not be sad when you give, and you should not give because you feel forced to give. God loves the person who gives happily. And God can give you more blessings than you need. Then you will always have plenty of everything—enough to give to every good work.

2 Corinthians 9:6–8

In all the work you are doing, work the best you can. Work as if you were doing it for the Lord, not for people. Remember that you will receive your reward from the Lord, which he promised to his people. You are serving the Lord Christ.

Colossians 3:23–24

Jesus said, "I tell you the truth, all those who have left houses, brothers, sisters, mother, father, children, or farms for me and for the Good News will get more than they left. Here in this world they will have a hundred times more homes, brothers, sisters, mothers, children, and fields. And with those things, they will also suffer for their belief. But in the age that is coming they will have life forever."

Mark 10:29–30

People should think of us as servants of Christ, the ones God has trusted with his secrets. Now in this way those who are trusted with something valuable must show they are worthy of that trust.

1 Corinthians 4:1–2

If I preach because it is my own choice, I have a

reward. But if I preach and it is not my choice to do so, I am only doing the duty that was given to me. So what reward do I get? This is my reward: that when I tell the Good News I can offer it freely. I do not use my full rights in my work of preaching the Good News. I am free and belong to no one. But I make myself a slave to all people to win as many as I can.

1 Corinthians 9:17–19

Each of you has received a gift to use to serve others. Be good servants of God's various gifts of grace. Anyone who speaks should speak words from God. Anyone who serves should serve with the strength God gives so that in everything God will be praised through Jesus Christ. Power and glory belong to him forever and ever. Amen.

1 Peter 4:10–11

Nothing in all the world can be hidden from God. Everything is clear and lies open before him, and to him we must explain the way we have lived.

Hebrews 4:13

Don't store treasures for yourselves here on earth where moths and rust will destroy them and thieves can break in and steal them. But store your treasures in heaven where they cannot be destroyed by moths or rust and where thieves cannot break in and steal them. Your heart will be where your treasure is.

Matthew 6:19–21

Give, and you will receive. You will be given much.

Pressed down, shaken together, and running over, it will spill into your lap. The way you give to others is the way God will give to you.

Luke 6:38

The thing you should want most is God's kingdom and doing what God wants. Then all these other things you need will be given to you.

Matthew 6:33

Obey the Lord your God so that all these blessings will come and stay with you: You will be blessed in the city and blessed in the country. Your basket and your kitchen will be blessed. You will be blessed when you come in and when you go out. The Lord will help you defeat the enemies that come to fight you. They will attack you from one direction, but they will run from you in seven directions. The Lord your God will bless you with full barns, and he will bless everything you do. He will bless the land he is giving you. The Lord will open up his heavenly storehouse so that the skies send rain on your land at the right time, and he will bless everything you do. You will lend to other nations, but you will not need to borrow from them. The Lord will make you like the head and not like the tail; you will be on top and not on bottom. But you must obey the commands of the Lord your God that I am giving you today, being careful to keep them.

Deuteronomy 28:2–3, 5–8, 12–13

Some people give much but get back even more. Others don't give what they should and end up poor. Whoever gives to others will get richer; those who help others will themselves be helped.

Proverbs 11:24–25

Always remember what is written in the Book of the Teachings. Study it day and night to be sure to obey everything that is written there. If you do this, you will be wise and successful in everything.

Joshua 1:8

Whoever can be trusted with a little can also be trusted with a lot, and whoever is dishonest with a little is dishonest with a lot. If you cannot be trusted with worldly riches, then who will trust you with true riches? And if you cannot be trusted with things that belong to someone else, who will give you things of your own? No servant can serve two masters. The servant will hate one master and love the other, or will follow one master and refuse to follow the other. You cannot serve both God and worldly riches.

Luke 16:10–13

When we have the opportunity to help anyone, we should do it. But we should give special attention to those who are in the family of believers.

Galatians 6:10

Our only goal is to please God whether we live here or there, because we must all stand before Christ to be judged. Each of us will receive what we should get—good or bad—for the things we did in the earthly body.

2 Corinthians 5:9–10

Be wise in the way you act with people who are not believers, making the most of every opportunity. When you talk, you should always be kind and pleasant so you will be able to answer everyone in the way you should.

Colossians 4:5–6

WHAT THE BIBLE HAS TO SAY
ABOUT

Satan

Control yourselves and be careful! The devil, your enemy, goes around like a roaring lion looking for someone to eat. Refuse to give in to him, by standing strong in your faith.

1 Peter 5:8–9a

So give yourselves completely to God. Stand against the devil, and the devil will run from you. Come near to God, and God will come near to you. You sinners, clean sin out of your lives. You who are trying to follow God and the world at the same time, make your thinking pure.

James 4:7–8

Finally, be strong in the Lord and in his great power. Put on the full armor of God so that you can fight against the devil's evil tricks. Our fight is not against people on earth but against the rulers and authorities and the powers of this world's darkness, against the spiritual powers of evil in the heavenly world. That is why you need to put on God's full armor. Then on the day of evil you will be able to stand strong. And when you have finished the whole fight, you will still be standing. So stand strong, with the belt of truth tied around your waist and the protection of right living on your chest. On your feet wear the

Good News of peace to help you stand strong. And also use the shield of faith with which you can stop all the burning arrows of the Evil One. Accept God's salvation as your helmet, and take the sword of the Spirit, which is the word of God. Pray in the Spirit at all times with all kinds of prayers, asking for everything you need. To do this you must always be ready and never give up. Always pray for all God's people.

Ephesians 6:10–18

But we see Jesus, who for a short time was made lower than the angels. And now he is wearing a crown of glory and honor because he suffered and died. And by God's grace, he died for everyone. God is the One who made all things, and all things are for his glory. He wanted to have many children share his glory, so he made the One who leads people to salvation perfect through suffering. Since these children are people with physical bodies, Jesus himself became like them. He did this so that, by dying, he could destroy the one who has the power of death—the devil—and free those who were like slaves all their lives because of their fear of death.

Hebrews 2:9–10, 14–15

All of God lives in Christ fully (even when Christ was on earth), and you have a full and true life in Christ, who is ruler over all rulers and powers. God stripped the spiritual rulers and powers of their authority. With the cross, he won the victory and showed the world that they were powerless.

Colossians 2:9–10, 15

God has freed us from the power of darkness, and he brought us into the kingdom of his dear Son.

Colossians 1:13

The LORD is like a strong tower; those who do right can run to him for safety.

Proverbs 18:10

The God who brings peace will soon defeat Satan and give you power over him. The grace of our Lord Jesus be with you.

Romans 16:20

Then I heard a loud voice in heaven saying: "The salvation and the power and the kingdom of our God and the authority of his Christ have now come. The accuser of our brothers and sisters, who accused them day and night before our God, has been thrown down. And our brothers and sisters defeated him by the blood of the Lamb's death and by the message they preached. They did not love their lives so much that they were afraid of death."

Revelation 12:10–11

My dear friends, many false prophets have gone out into the world. So do not believe every spirit, but test the spirits to see if they are from God. This is how you can know God's Spirit: Every spirit who confesses that Jesus Christ came to earth as a human is from God. And every spirit who refuses to say this about Jesus is not from God. It is the spirit of the enemy of Christ, which you have heard is coming, and now he is already in the world. My dear children, you belong to God and have defeated them; because God's Spirit, who is in you, is greater than the devil, who is in the world. And they belong to the world, so what they say is from the world, and the world listens to them. But we belong to God, and those who know God listen to us. But those who are not from God do not listen to us. That is how we know the Spirit that is true and the spirit that is false.

1 John 4:1–6

When the seventy-two came back, they were very happy and said, "Lord, even the demons obeyed us when we used your name!" Jesus said, "I saw Satan fall like lightning from heaven. Listen, I have given you power to walk on snakes and scorpions, power that is greater than the enemy has. So nothing will hurt you. But you should not be happy because the spirits obey you but because your names are written in heaven."

Luke 10:17–20

And those who believe will be able to do these things as proof: They will use my name to force out demons. They will speak in new languages. They will pick up snakes and drink poison without being hurt. They will touch the sick, and the sick will be healed.

Mark 16:17–18

But if I use the power of God's Spirit to force out demons, then the kingdom of God has come to you.

Matthew 12:28

We do live in the world, but we do not fight in the same way the world fights. We fight with weapons that are different from those the world uses. Our weapons have power from God that can destroy the enemy's strong places. We destroy people's arguments and every proud thing that raises itself against the knowledge of God. We capture every thought and make it give up and obey Christ.

2 Corinthians 10:3–5

Dear children, do not let anyone lead you the wrong way. Christ is all that is right. So to be like Christ a person must do what is right. The devil has been sinning since the beginning, so anyone who continues to sin belongs to the devil. The Son of God came for this purpose: to destroy the devil's work.

1 John 3:7–8

I write to you, dear children, because your sins are forgiven through Christ. I write to you, children, because you know the Father. I write to you, parents, because you know the One who existed from the beginning. I write to you, young people, because you are strong; the teaching of God lives in you, and you have defeated the Evil One.

1 John 2:12, 14

WHAT THE BIBLE HAS TO SAY
ABOUT

Spiritual Warfare

Finally, be strong in the Lord and in his great power. Put on the full armor of God so that you can fight against the devil's evil tricks. Our fight is not against people on earth but against the rulers and authorities and the powers of this world's darkness, against the spiritual powers of evil in the heavenly world.

Ephesians 6:10–12

Share in the troubles we have like a good soldier of Christ Jesus. A soldier wants to please the enlisting officer, so no one serving in the army wastes time with everyday matters.

2 Timothy 2:3–4

Pray in the Spirit at all times with all kinds of prayers, asking for everything you need. To do this you must always be ready and never give up. Always pray for all God's people.

Ephesians 6:18

That is why you need to put on God's full armor. Then on the day of evil you will be able to stand strong. And when you have finished the whole fight, you will still be standing. So stand strong, with the belt of truth tied around your waist and the protection of right living on your chest. On your feet wear the

Good News of peace to help you stand strong. And also use the shield of faith with which you can stop all the burning arrows of the Evil One. Accept God's salvation as your helmet, and take the sword of the Spirit, which is the word of God.

Ephesians 6:13–17

The God who brings peace will soon defeat Satan and give you power over him. The grace of our Lord Jesus be with you.

Romans 16:20

God will do what is right. He will give trouble to those who trouble you. And he will give rest to you who are troubled and to us also when the Lord Jesus appears with burning fire from heaven with his powerful angels.

2 Thessalonians 1:6–7

Don't let anyone among you offer a son or daughter as a sacrifice in the fire. Don't let anyone use magic or witchcraft, or try to explain the meaning of signs. Don't let anyone try to control others with magic, and don't let them be mediums or try to talk with the spirits of dead people. The LORD hates anyone who does these things. Because the other nations do these things, the LORD your God will force them out of the land ahead of you. But you must be innocent in the presence of the LORD your God. The nations you will force out listen to people who use magic and witchcraft, but the LORD your God will not let you do those things.

Deuteronomy 18:10–14

But we belong to the day, so we should control ourselves. We should wear faith and love to protect us, and the hope of salvation should be our helmet.

1 Thessalonians 5:8

After his soul suffers many things, he will see life and be satisfied. My good servant will make many people right with God; he will carry away their sins. For this reason I will make him a great man among people, and he will share in all things with those who are strong. He willingly gave his life and was treated like a criminal. But he carried away the sins of many people and asked forgiveness for those who sinned.

Isaiah 53:11–12

We do live in the world, but we do not fight in the same way the world fights. We fight with weapons that are different from those the world uses. Our weapons have power from God that can destroy the enemy's strong places. We destroy people's arguments and every proud thing that raises itself against the knowledge of God. We capture every thought and make it give up and obey Christ.

2 Corinthians 10:34

The Lord will save me when anyone tries to hurt me, and he will bring me safely to his heavenly Kingdom. Glory forever and ever be the Lord's.

2 Timothy 4:18

Control yourselves and be careful! The devil, your enemy, goes around like a roaring lion looking for someone to eat.

1 Peter 5:8

Since these children are people with physical bodies, Jesus himself became like them. He did this so that, by dying, he could destroy the one who has the power of death—the devil— and free those who were like slaves all their lives because of their fear of death.

Hebrews 2:14–15

So give yourselves completely to God. Stand against the devil, and the devil will run from you.

James 4:7

Hell

If your right eye causes you to sin, take it out and throw it away. It is better to lose one part of your body than to have your whole body thrown into hell. If your right hand causes you to sin, cut it off and throw it away. It is better to lose one part of your body than for your whole body to go into hell.

Matthew 5:29–30

Then the King will say to those on his left, "Go away from me. You will be punished. Go into the fire that burns forever that was prepared for the devil and his angels."

Matthew 25:41

But cowards, those who refuse to believe, who do evil things, who kill, who sin sexually, who do evil magic, who worship idols, and who tell lies— all these will have a place in the lake of burning sulfur. This is the second death.

Revelation 21:8

Then a third angel followed the first two angels, saying in a loud voice: "If anyone worships the beast and his idol and gets the beast's mark on the forehead or on the hand, that one also will drink the wine of God's anger, which is prepared with all its strength in the cup of his anger. And that person will be put in pain with burning sulfur before the holy angels and the Lamb. And the smoke from their burning pain will rise forever and ever. There will be no rest, day or night, for those who worship the beast and his idol or who get the mark of his name."

Revelation 14:9–11

Don't be afraid of people, who can kill the body but cannot kill the soul. The only one you should fear is the one who can destroy the soul and the body in hell.

Matthew 10:28

And the tongue is like a fire. It is a whole world of evil among the parts of our bodies. The tongue spreads its evil through the whole body. The tongue is set on fire by hell, and it starts a fire that influences all of life.

James 3:6

And he will give rest to you who are troubled and to us also when the Lord Jesus appears with burning fire from heaven with his powerful angels. Then he will punish those who do not know God and who do not obey the Good News about our Lord Jesus Christ. Those people will be punished with a destruction that continues forever. They will be kept away from the Lord and from his great power.

2 Thessalonians 1:7–9

These people will go off to be punished forever, but the good people will go to live forever.

Matthew 25:46

The Son of Man will send out his angels, and they will gather out of his kingdom all who cause sin and all who do evil. The angels will throw them into the blazing furnace, where the people will cry and grind their teeth with pain.

Matthew 13:41–42

When angels sinned, God did not let them go free without punishment. He sent them to hell and put them in caves of darkness where they are being held for judgment.

2 Peter 2:4

In hell the worm does not die; the fire is never put out. Every person will be salted with fire.

Mark 9:48–49

WHAT THE BIBLE HAS TO SAY ABOUT

The Return of Christ

Brothers and sisters, we want you to know about those Christians who have died so you will not be sad, as others who have no hope. We believe that Jesus died and that he rose again. So, because of him, God will raise with Jesus those who have died. What we tell you now is the Lord's own message. We who are living when the Lord comes again will not go before those who have already died. The Lord himself will come down from heaven with a loud command, with the voice of the archangel, and with the trumpet call of God. And those who have died believing in Christ will rise first. After that, we who are still alive will be gathered up with them in the clouds to meet the Lord in the air. And we will be with the Lord forever. So encourage each other with these words.

1 Thessalonians 4:13–18

But look! I tell you this secret: We will not all sleep in death, but we will all be changed. It will take only a second— as quickly as an eye blinks— when the last trumpet sounds. The trumpet will sound, and those who have died will be raised to live forever, and we will all be changed. This body that can be destroyed must clothe itself with something that can never be destroyed. And this body that dies must clothe itself with something that can never die. So this body that can be destroyed will clothe itself with that which can never be destroyed, and this body that dies will clothe itself with that which can never die. When this happens, this Scripture will be made true: "Death is destroyed forever in victory." "Death, where is your victory? Death, where is your pain?" Death's power to hurt is sin, and the power of sin is the law. But we thank God! He gives us the victory through our Lord Jesus Christ.

1 Corinthians 15:51–57

They said, "Men of Galilee, why are you standing here looking into the sky? Jesus, whom you saw taken up from you into heaven, will come back in the same way you saw him go."

Acts 1:11

That is the way we should live, because God's grace that can save everyone has come. It teaches us not to live against God nor to do the evil things the world wants to do. Instead, that grace teaches us to live now in a wise and right way and in a way that shows we serve God. We should live like that while we wait for our great hope and the coming of the glory of our great God and Savior Jesus Christ.

Titus 2:11–13

It is most important for you to understand what will happen in the last days. People will laugh at you. They will live doing the evil things they want to do.

They will say, "Jesus promised to come again. Where is he? Our fathers have died, but the world continues the way it has been since it was made." But do not forget this one thing, dear friends: To the Lord one day is as a thousand years, and a thousand years is as one day. The Lord is not slow in doing what he promised—the way some people understand slowness. But God is being patient with you. He does not want anyone to be lost, but he wants all people to change their hearts and lives. But the day of the Lord will come like a thief. The skies will disappear with a loud noise. Everything in them will be destroyed by fire, and the earth and everything in it will be burned up. In that way everything will be destroyed. So what kind of people should you be? You should live holy lives and serve God, as you wait for and look forward to the coming of the day of God. When that day comes, the skies will be destroyed with fire, and everything in them will melt with heat. But God made a promise to us, and we are waiting for a new heaven and a new earth where goodness lives.

2 Peter 3:3–4, 8–13

When the Son of Man comes, he will be seen by everyone, like lightning flashing from the east to the west. Soon after the trouble of those days, the sun will grow dark, and the moon will not give its light. The stars will fall from the sky. And the powers of the heavens will be shaken. At that time, the sign of the Son of Man will appear in the sky. Then all the peoples of the world will cry. They will see the Son of Man coming on clouds in the sky with great power and glory. He will use a loud trumpet to send his angels all around the earth, and they will gather his chosen people from every part of the world.

Matthew 24:27, 29–31

I give you a command in the presence of God and Christ Jesus, the One who will judge the living and the dead, and by his coming and his kingdom: Preach the Good News. Be ready at all times, and tell people what they need to do. Tell them when they are wrong. Encourage them with great patience and careful teaching, because the time will come when people will not listen to the true teaching but will find many more teachers who please them by saying the things they want to hear. They will stop listening to the truth and will begin to follow false stories. But you should control yourself at all times, accept troubles, do the work of telling the Good News, and complete all the duties of a servant of God. My life is being given as an offering to God, and the time has come for me to leave this life. I have fought the good fight, I have finished the race, I have kept the faith. Now, a crown is being held for me—a crown for being right with God. The Lord, the judge who judges rightly, will give the crown to me on that day—not only to me but to all those who have waited with love for him to come again.

2 Timothy 4:1–8

I tell you the truth, all these things will happen while the people of this time are still living. Earth and sky will be destroyed, but the words I have said will never be destroyed.

Matthew 24:34–35

Dear friends, now we are children of God, and we have not yet been shown what we will be in the future. But we know that when Christ comes again, we will be like him, because we will see him as he really is. Christ is pure, and all who have this hope in Christ keep themselves pure like Christ.

1 John 3:2–3

There will be signs in the sun, moon, and stars. On earth, nations will be afraid and confused because of the roar and fury of the sea. People will be so afraid they will faint, wondering what is happening to the world, because the powers of the heavens will be shaken. Then people will see the Son of Man coming in a cloud with power and great glory. When these things begin to happen, look up and hold your heads high, because the time when God will free you is near!

Luke 21:25–28

Later, as Jesus was sitting on the Mount of Olives, his followers came to be alone with him. They said, "Tell us, when will these things happen? And what will be the sign that it is time for you to come again and for this age to end?" Jesus answered, "Be careful that no one fools you. Many will come in my name, saying, 'I am the Christ,' and they will fool many people. You will hear about wars and stories of wars that are coming, but don't be afraid. These things must happen before the end comes. Nations will fight against other nations; kingdoms will fight against other kingdoms. There will be times when there is no food for people to eat, and there will be earthquakes in different places. These things are like the first pains when something new is about to be born. Then people will arrest you, hand you over to be hurt, and kill you. They will hate you because you believe in me. At that time, many will lose their faith, and they will turn against each other and hate each other. Many false prophets will come and cause many people to believe lies. There will be more and more evil in the world, so most people will stop showing their love for each other. But those people who keep their faith until the end will be saved. The Good News about God's kingdom will be preached in all the world, to every nation. Then the end will come."

Matthew 24:3–14

Remember this! In the last days there will be many troubles, because people will love themselves, love money, brag, and be proud. They will say evil things against others and will not obey their parents or be thankful or be the kind of people God wants. They will not love others, will refuse to forgive, will gossip, and will not control themselves. They will be cruel, will hate what is good, will turn against their friends, and will do foolish things without thinking. They will be conceited, will love pleasure instead of God, and will act as if they serve God but will not have his power. Stay away from those people.

2 Timothy 3:1–5

Now the Holy Spirit clearly says that in the later times some people will stop believing the faith. They will follow spirits that lie and teachings of demons. Such teachings come from the false words of liars whose consciences are destroyed as if by a hot iron. They forbid people to marry and tell them not to eat certain foods which God created to be eaten with thanks by people who believe and know the truth. Everything God made is good, and nothing should be refused if it is accepted with thanks, because it is made holy by what God has said and by prayer.

1 Timothy 4:1–5

No one knows when that day or time will be, not the angels in heaven, not even the Son. Only the Father knows. When the Son of Man comes, it will be like what happened during Noah's time. In those days before the flood, people were eating and drinking, marrying and giving their children to be married, until the day Noah entered the boat. They knew nothing about what was happening until the flood came and destroyed them. It will be the same when the Son of Man comes. Two men will be in the field. One will be taken, and the other will be left. Two women will be grinding grain with a mill. One will be taken, and the other will be left. So always be ready, because you don't know the day your Lord will come. Remember this: If the owner of the house knew what time of night a thief was coming, the owner would watch and not let the thief break in. So you also must be ready, because the Son of Man will come at a time you don't expect him.

Matthew 24:36–44

Jesus said, "Don't let your hearts be troubled. Trust in God, and trust in me. There are many rooms in my Father's house; I would not tell you this if it were not true. I am going there to prepare a place for you. After I go and prepare a place for you, I will come back and take you to be with me so that you may be where I am. You know the way to the place where I am going."

John 14:1–4

The Unsaved

All have sinned and are not good enough for God's glory, and all need to be made right with God by his grace, which is a free gift. They need to be made free from sin through Jesus Christ.

Romans 3:23–24

Sin came into the world because of what one man did, and with sin came death. This is why everyone must die—because everyone sinned.

Romans 5:12

When people sin, they earn what sin pays— death. But God gives us a free gift—life forever in Christ Jesus our Lord.

Romans 6:23

God's anger is shown from heaven against all the evil and wrong things people do. By their own evil lives they hide the truth. God shows his anger because some knowledge of him has been made clear to them. Yes, God has shown himself to them. There are things about him that people cannot see—his eternal power and all the things that make him God. But since the beginning of the world those things have been easy to understand by what God has made. So people have no excuse for the bad things they do.

Romans 1:18–20

But God shows his great love for us in this way: Christ died for us while we were still sinners. So through Christ we will surely be saved from God's anger, because we have been made right with God by the blood of Christ's death.

Romans 5:8–9

Jesus said to his followers, "Go everywhere in the world, and tell the Good News to everyone. Anyone who believes and is baptized will be saved, but anyone who does not believe will be punished."

Mark 16:15–16

The Lord has put his Spirit in me, because he appointed me to tell the Good News to the poor. He has sent me to tell the captives they are free and to tell the blind that they can see again. God sent me to free those who have been treated unfairly and to announce the time when the Lord will show his kindness.

Luke 4:18–19

The Lord is not slow in doing what he promised— the way some people understand slowness. But God is being patient with you. He does not want anyone to be lost, but he wants all people to change their hearts and lives.

2 Peter 3:9

God did not send his Son into the world to judge the world guilty, but to save the world through him.

John 3:17

I have not come to invite good people but sinners to change their hearts and lives.

Luke 5:32

The Son of Man came to find lost people and save them.

Luke 19:10

Jesus answered, "I tell you the truth, unless one is born again, he cannot be in God's kingdom."

John 3:3

God loved the world so much that he gave his one and only Son so that whoever believes in him may not be lost, but have eternal life.

John 3:16

They said to him, "Believe in the Lord Jesus and you will be saved—you and all the people in your house."

Acts 16:31

WHAT THE BIBLE HAS TO SAY ABOUT

The Qualities of a Christian

You are God's children whom he loves, so try to be like him.

Ephesians 5:1

I am the true vine; my Father is the gardener. He cuts off every branch of mine that does not produce fruit. And he trims and cleans every branch that produces fruit so that it will produce even more fruit. You are already clean because of the words I have spoken to you. Remain in me, and I will remain in you. A branch cannot produce fruit alone but must remain in the vine. In the same way, you cannot produce fruit alone but must remain in me.

John 15:1–4

We must not become tired of doing good. We will receive our harvest of eternal life at the right time if we do not give up. When we have the opportunity to help anyone, we should do it. But we should give special attention to those who are in the family of believers.

Galatians 6:9–10

God has chosen you and made you his holy people. He loves you. So always do these things: Show mercy to others, be kind, humble, gentle, and patient. Get along with each other, and forgive each other. If someone does wrong to you, forgive that person because the Lord forgave you. Do all these things; but most important, love each other. Love is what holds you all together in perfect unity. Let the peace that Christ gives control your thinking, because you were all called together in one body to have peace. Always be thankful. Let the teaching of Christ live in you richly. Use all wisdom to teach and instruct each other by singing psalms, hymns, and spiritual songs with thankfulness in your hearts to God. Everything you do or say should be done to obey Jesus your Lord. And in all you do, give thanks to God the Father through Jesus.

Colossians 3:12–17

We live by what we believe, not by what we can see.

2 Corinthians 5:7

Share in the troubles we have like a good soldier of Christ Jesus.

2 Timothy 2:3

Give my greetings to Priscilla and Aquila, who work together with me in Christ Jesus and who risked their own lives to save my life. I am thankful to them, and all the non-Jewish churches are thankful as well. Also, greet for me the church that meets at their house. Greetings to my dear friend Epenetus, who was the first person in the country of Asia to follow Christ.

Romans 16:3–5

Then someone came and told them, "Listen! The men you put in jail are standing in the Temple teaching the people." Then the captain and his men went out and brought the apostles back. But the soldiers did not use force, because they were afraid the people would stone them to death. The soldiers brought the apostles to the meeting and made them stand before the Jewish leaders. The high priest questioned them, saying, "We gave you strict orders not to continue teaching in that name. But look, you have filled Jerusalem with your teaching and are trying to make us responsible for this man's death." Peter and the other apostles answered, "We must obey God, not human authority!"

Acts 5:25–29

LORD, who may enter your Holy Tent? Who may live on your holy mountain? Only those who are innocent and who do what is right. Such people speak the truth from their hearts and do not tell lies about others. They do no wrong to their neighbors and do not gossip. They do not respect hateful people but honor those who honor the LORD. They keep their promises to their neighbors, even when it hurts. They do not charge interest on money they lend and do not take money to hurt innocent people. Whoever does all these things will never be destroyed.

Psalm 15:1–5

Truth from the Bible about...

TRUTH FROM THE BIBLE ABOUT
Forgiving Others

Yes, if you forgive others for their sins, your Father in heaven will also forgive you for your sins. But if you don't forgive others, your Father in heaven will not forgive your sins.

Matthew 6:14–15

Then Peter came to Jesus and asked, "Lord, when my fellow believer sins against me, how many times must I forgive him? Should I forgive him as many as seven times?" Jesus answered, "I tell you, you must forgive him more than seven times. You must forgive him even if he does wrong to you seventy-seven times."

Matthew 18:21–22

So be careful! If another follower sins, warn him, and if he is sorry and stops sinning, forgive him. If he sins against you seven times in one day and says that he is sorry each time, forgive him.

Luke 17:3–4

When you are praying, if you are angry with someone, forgive him so that your Father in heaven will also forgive your sins.

Mark 11:25

Get along with each other, and forgive each other. If someone does wrong to you, forgive that person because the Lord forgave you.

Colossians 3:13

But I say to you, love your enemies. Pray for those who hurt you.

Matthew 5:44

Do not do wrong to repay a wrong, and do not insult to repay an insult. But repay with a blessing, because you yourselves were called to do this so that you might receive a blessing. The Scripture says, "A person must do these things to enjoy life and have many happy days. He must not say evil things, and he must not tell lies."

1 Peter 3:9–10

Do not be bitter or angry or mad. Never shout angrily or say things to hurt others. Never do anything evil. Be kind and loving to each other, and forgive each other just as God forgave you in Christ.

Ephesians 4:31–32

Brothers and sisters, I know that I have not yet reached that goal, but there is one thing I always do. Forgetting the past and straining toward what is ahead, I keep trying to reach the goal and get the prize for which God called me through Christ to the life above.

Philippians 3:13–14

The Lord says, "Forget what happened before, and do not think about the past. I, I am the One who forgives all your sins, for my sake; I will not remember your sins."

Isaiah 43:18, 25

A person might have to suffer even when it is unfair, but if he thinks of God and stands the pain, God is pleased. If you are beaten for doing wrong, there is no reason to praise you for being patient in your punishment. But if you suffer for doing good, and you are patient, then God is pleased. This is what you were called to do, because Christ suffered for you and gave you an example to follow. So you should do as he did. "He had never sinned, and he had never lied." People insulted Christ, but he did not insult them in return. Christ suffered, but he did not threaten. He let God, the One who judges rightly, take care of him.

1 Peter 2:19–23

Those who are treated badly for doing good are happy, because the kingdom of heaven belongs to them. People will insult you and hurt you. They will lie and say all kinds of evil things about you because you follow me. But when they do, you will be happy. Rejoice and be glad, because you have a great reward waiting for you in heaven. People did the same evil things to the prophets who lived before you.

Matthew 5:10–12

We know that God said, "I will punish those who do wrong; I will repay them." And he also said, "The Lord will judge his people."

Hebrews 10:30

My friends, do not be surprised at the terrible trouble which now comes to test you. Do not think that something strange is happening to you. But be happy that you are sharing in Christ's sufferings so that you will be happy and full of joy when Christ comes again in glory. When people insult you because you follow Christ, you are blessed, because the glorious Spirit, the Spirit of God, is with you.

1 Peter 4:12–14

Do not let evil defeat you, but defeat evil by doing good.

Romans 12:21

TRUTH FROM THE BIBLE ABOUT
Christian Fellowship

We announce to you what we have seen and heard, because we want you also to have fellowship with us. Our fellowship is with God the Father and with his Son, Jesus Christ. But if we live in the light, as God is in the light, we can share fellowship with each other. Then the blood of Jesus, God's Son, cleanses us from every sin.

1 John 1:3, 7

Live a life of love just as Christ loved us and gave himself for us as a sweet-smelling offering and sacrifice to God. Speak to each other with psalms, hymns, and spiritual songs, singing and making music in your hearts to the Lord. Always give thanks to God the Father for everything, in the name of our Lord Jesus Christ.

Ephesians 5:2, 19–20

Let the teaching of Christ live in you richly. Use all wisdom to teach and instruct each other by singing psalms, hymns, and spiritual songs with thankfulness in your hearts to God. Everything you do or say should be done to obey Jesus your Lord. And in all you do, give thanks to God the Father through Jesus.

Colossians 3:16-17

I want them to be strengthened and joined together

with love so that they may be rich in their understanding. This leads to their knowing fully God's secret, that is, Christ himself.

Colossians 2:2

Then those who honored the LORD spoke with each other, and the LORD listened and heard them. The names of those who honored the LORD and respected him were written in his presence in a book to be remembered. The LORD All-Powerful says, "They belong to me; on that day they will be my very own. As a parent shows mercy to his child who serves him, I will show mercy to my people. You will again see the difference between good and evil people, between those who serve God and those who don't."

Malachi 3:16–18

That same day two of Jesus' followers were going to a town named Emmaus, about seven miles from Jerusalem. They were talking about everything that had happened. While they were talking and discussing, Jesus himself came near and began walking with them.

Luke 24:13–15

Now you who are not Jewish are not foreigners or strangers any longer, but are citizens together with God's holy people. You belong to God's family. You are like a building that was built on the foundation of the apostles and prophets. Christ Jesus himself is the most important stone in that building, and that whole building is joined together in Christ. He makes it grow and become a holy temple in the Lord. And in Christ you, too, are being built together with the Jews into a place where God lives through the Spirit.

Ephesians 2:19–22

Does your life in Christ give you strength? Does his love comfort you? Do we share together in the spirit? Do you have mercy and kindness? If so, make me very happy by having the same thoughts, sharing the same love, and having one mind and purpose.

Philippians 2:1–2

We had a good friendship and walked together to God's Temple.

Psalm 55:14

I am coming to you; I will not stay in the world any longer. But they are still in the world. Holy Father, keep them safe by the power of your name, the name you gave me, so that they will be one, just as you and I are one. Father, I pray that they can be one. As you are in me and I am in you, I pray that they can also be one in us. Then the world will believe that you sent me. I have given these people the glory that you gave me so that they can be one, just as you and I are one. I will be in them and you will be in me so that they will be completely one. Then the world will know that you sent me and that you loved them just as much as you loved me.

John 17:11, 21–23

When the day of Pentecost came, they were all

together in one place. They spent their time learning the apostles' teaching, sharing, breaking bread, and praying together. The believers met together in the Temple every day. They ate together in their homes, happy to share their food with joyful hearts . They praised God and were liked by all the people. Every day the Lord added those who were being saved to the group of believers.

Acts 2:1, 42, 46–47

Patience and encouragement come from God. And I pray that God will help you all agree with each other the way Christ Jesus wants. Then you will all be joined together, and you will give glory to God the Father of our Lord Jesus Christ. Christ accepted you, so you should accept each other, which will bring glory to God.

Romans 15:5–7

I beg you, brothers and sisters, by the name of our Lord Jesus Christ that all of you agree with each other and not be split into groups. I beg that you be completely joined together by having the same kind of thinking and the same purpose.

1 Corinthians 1:10

By helping each other with your troubles, you truly obey the law of Christ. When we have the opportunity to help anyone, we should do it. But we should give special attention to those who are in the family of believers.

Galatians 6:2, 10

I thank my God every time I remember you, always praying with joy for all of you. Only one thing concerns me: Be sure that you live in a way that brings honor to the Good News of Christ. Then whether I come and visit you or am away from you, I will hear that you are standing strong with one purpose, that you work together as one for the faith of the Good News.

Philippians 1:3–4, 27

Let us come near to God with a sincere heart and a sure faith, because we have been made free from a guilty conscience, and our bodies have been washed with pure water. Let us hold firmly to the hope that we have confessed, because we can trust God to do what he promised. Let us think about each other and help each other to show love and do good deeds. You should not stay away from the church meetings, as some are doing, but you should meet together and encourage each other. Do this even more as you see the day coming.

Hebrews 10:22–25

TRUTH FROM THE BIBLE ABOUT
Your Responsibility

Jesus said to his followers, "Go everywhere in the world, and tell the Good News to everyone."

Mark 16:15

But when the Holy Spirit comes to you, you will receive power. You will be my witnesses—in Jerusalem, in all of Judea, in Samaria, and in every part of the world.

Acts 1:8

You are the salt of the earth. But if the salt loses its salty taste, it cannot be made salty again. It is good for nothing, except to be thrown out and walked on. You are the light that gives light to the world. A city that is built on a hill cannot be hidden. And people don't hide a light under a bowl. They put it on a lampstand so the light shines for all the people in the house. In the same way, you should be a light for other people. Live so that they will see the good things you do and will praise your Father in heaven.

Matthew 5:13–16

"I was hungry, and you gave me food. I was thirsty, and you gave me something to drink. I was alone and away from home, and you invited me into your house. I was without clothes, and you gave me something to wear. I was sick, and you cared for me. I was in prison, and you visited me." Then the good people will answer, "Lord, when did we see you hungry and give you food, or thirsty and give you something to drink? When did we see you alone and away from home and invite you into our house? When did we see you without clothes and give you something to wear? When did we see you sick or in prison and care for you?" Then the King will answer, "I tell you the truth, anything you did for even the least of my people here, you also did for me."

Matthew 25:35–40

Those who give one of these little ones a cup of cold water because they are my followers will truly get their reward.

Matthew 10:42

Whoever does not care for his own relatives, especially his own family members, has turned against the faith and is worse than someone who does not believe in God.

1 Timothy 5:8

Train children how to live right, and when they are old, they will not change.

Proverbs 22:6

God is fair; he will not forget the work you did and the love you showed for him by helping his people. And he will remember that you are still helping them. We want each of you to go on with the same hard work all your lives so you will surely get what you hope for. We do not want you to become lazy.

Be like those who through faith and patience will receive what God has promised.

Hebrews 6:10–12

A brother or sister in Christ might need clothes or food. If you say to that person, "God be with you! I hope you stay warm and get plenty to eat," but you do not give what that person needs, your words are worth nothing. In the same way, faith that is alone— that does nothing—is dead.

James 2:15–17

The people asked John, "Then what should we do?" John answered, "If you have two shirts, share with the person who does not have one. If you have food, share that also."

Luke 3:10–11

Brothers and sisters, if someone in your group does something wrong, you who are spiritual should go to that person and gently help make him right again. But be careful, because you might be tempted to sin, too. By helping each other with your troubles, you truly obey the law of Christ. If anyone thinks he is important when he really is not, he is only fooling himself. Each person should judge his own actions and not compare himself with others. Then he can be proud for what he himself has done. Each person must be responsible for himself. Anyone who is learning the teaching of God should share all the good things he has with his teacher.

Galatians 6:1–6

This is how we know what real love is: Jesus gave his life for us. So we should give our lives for our brothers and sisters. Suppose someone has enough to live and sees a brother or sister in need, but does not help. Then God's love is not living in that person. My children, we should love people not only with words and talk, but by our actions and true caring. And God gives us what we ask for because we obey God's commands and do what pleases him. This is what God commands: that we believe in his Son, Jesus Christ, and that we love each other, just as he commanded.

1 John 3:16–18, 22–23

Always remember these commands I give you today. Teach them to your children, and talk about them when you sit at home and walk along the road, when you lie down and when you get up. Write them down and tie them to your hands as a sign. Tie them on your forehead to remind you, and write them on your doors and gates.

Deuteronomy 6:6–9

Love the LORD your God and always obey his orders, rules, laws, and commands. Remember my words with your whole being. Write them down and tie them to your hands as a sign; tie them on your foreheads to remind you. Teach them well to your children, talking about them when you sit at home and walk along the road, when you lie down and when you get up.

Deuteronomy 11:1, 18–19

Respecting the LORD and not being proud will bring you wealth, honor, and life.

Proverbs 22:4

Speaking God's Word

I tell you the truth, you can say to this mountain, "Go, fall into the sea." And if you have no doubts in your mind and believe that what you say will happen, God will do it for you.

Mark 11:23

The Lord said, "If your faith were the size of a mustard seed, you could say to this mulberry tree, 'Dig yourself up and plant yourself in the sea,' and it would obey you."

Luke 17:6

Jesus stood up and commanded the wind and said to the waves, "Quiet! Be still!" Then the wind stopped, and it became completely calm.

Mark 4:39

It is by faith we understand that the whole world was made by God's command so what we see was made by something that cannot be seen.

Hebrews 11:3

The things I taught were not from myself. The Father who sent me told me what to say and what to teach. And I know that eternal life comes from what the Father commands. So whatever I say is what the Father told me to say.

John 12:49–50

So the Lord said to me, "What they have said is good. So I will give them a prophet like you, who is one of their own people. I will tell him what to say, and he will tell them everything I command. This prophet will speak for me; anyone who does not listen when he speaks will answer to me."

Deuteronomy 18:17–19

This is what the Scripture says: "The word is near you; it is in your mouth and in your heart." That is the teaching of faith that we are telling. If you use your mouth to say, "Jesus is Lord," and if you believe in your heart that God raised Jesus from the dead, you will be saved. We believe with our hearts, and so we are made right with God. And we use our mouths to say that we believe, and so we are saved.

Romans 10:8–10

It is written in the Scriptures, "I believed, so I spoke." Our faith is like this, too. We believe and so we speak. God raised the Lord Jesus from the dead, and we know that God will also raise us with Jesus. God will bring us together with you, and we will stand before him.

2 Corinthians 4:13–14

Careless words stab like a sword, but wise words bring healing. The Lord hates those who tell lies, but is pleased with those who keep their promises.

Proverbs 12:18, 22

You who are his angels, praise the Lord. You are

the mighty warriors who do what he says and who obey his voice. You, his armies, praise the LORD; you are his servants who do what he wants. Everything the LORD has made should praise him in all the places he rules. My whole being, praise the LORD.

Psalm 103:20–22

The wise are known for their understanding. Their pleasant words make them better teachers. Wise people's minds tell them what to say, and that helps them be better teachers. Pleasant words are like a honeycomb, making people happy and healthy. Useless people make evil plans, and their words are like a burning fire.

Proverbs 16:21, 23–24, 27

Spoken words can be like deep water, but wisdom is like a flowing stream. The words of fools will ruin them; their own words will trap them. People will be rewarded for what they say; they will be rewarded by how they speak. What you say can mean life or death. Those who speak with care will be rewarded.

Proverbs 18:4, 7, 20–21

The mouth speaks the things that are in the heart. And I tell you that on the Judgment Day people will be responsible for every careless thing they have said. The words you have said will be used to judge you. Some of your words will prove you right, but some of your words will prove you guilty.

Matthew 12:34b, 36–37

People who think they are religious but say things they should not say are just fooling themselves. Their "religion" is worth nothing.

James 1:26

Let us hold firmly to the hope that we have confessed, because we can trust God to do what he promised.

Hebrews 10:23

People will be rewarded for what they say, but those who can't be trusted want only violence. Those who are careful about what they say protect their lives, but whoever speaks without thinking will be ruined.

Proverbs 13:2–3

TRUTH FROM THE BIBLE ABOUT
God's Will for Your Life

But if any of you needs wisdom, you should ask God for it. He is generous and enjoys giving to all people, so he will give you wisdom. But when you ask God, you must believe and not doubt. Anyone who doubts is like a wave in the sea, blown up and down by the wind.

James 1:5–6

The Lord says, "I will make you wise and show you where to go. I will guide you and watch over you."

Psalm 32:8

Your word is like a lamp for my feet and a light for my path. I will do what I have promised and obey your fair laws.

Psalm 119:105–106

My son, keep you father's commands, and don't forget your mother's teaching. They will guide you when you walk. They will guard you when you sleep. They will speak to you when you are awake. These commands are like a lamp; this teaching is like a light. And the correction that comes from them will help you have life.

Proverbs 6:20, 22–23

Always remember what is written in the Book of the Teachings. Study it day and night to be sure to obey everything that is written there. If you do this, you will be wise and successful in everything. Remember that I commanded you to be strong and brave. Don't be afraid, because the LORD your God will be with you everywhere you go.

Joshua 1:8–9

If you go the wrong way—to the right or to the left—you will hear a voice behind you saying, "This is the right way. You should go this way."

Isaiah 30:21

This God is our God forever and ever. He will guide us from now on.

Psalm 48:14

God wants you to be holy and to stay away from sexual sins. He wants each of you to learn to control your own body in a way that is holy and honorable. Also, do not wrong or cheat another Christian in this way. The Lord will punish people who do those things as we have already told you and warned you.

1 Thessalonians 4:3–4, 6

Always be joyful. Pray continually, and give thanks whatever happens. That is what God wants for you in Christ Jesus.

1 Thessalonians 5:16–18

In our prayers for you we always thank God, the Father of our Lord Jesus Christ, Because of this, since the day we heard about you, we have continued praying for you, asking God that you will know fully what he wants. We pray that you will also have great wisdom and understanding in spiritual things so that you will live the kind of life that honors and pleases the Lord in every way. You will produce fruit in every good work and grow in the knowledge of God.

Colossians 1:3, 9–10

Teach me to do what you want, because you are my God. Let your good Spirit lead me on level ground.

Psalm 143:10

First, I tell you to pray for all people, asking God for what they need and being thankful to him. This is good, and it pleases God our Savior, who wants all people to be saved and to know the truth.

1 Timothy 2:1, 3–4

Depend on the Lord in whatever you do, and your plans will succeed.

Proverbs 16:3

When a person's steps follow the Lord, God is pleased with his ways. If he stumbles, he will not fall, because the Lord holds his hand.

Psalm 37:23–24

You are my rock and my protection. For the good of your name, lead me and guide me. I give you my life. Save me, Lord, God of truth.

Psalm 31:3, 5

You saw our ancestors suffering in Egypt and heard them cry out at the Red Sea. You came down to Mount Sinai and spoke from heaven to our ancestors. You gave them fair rules and true teachings, good orders and commands. You gave your good Spirit to teach them. You gave them manna to eat and water when they were thirsty.

Nehemiah 9:9, 13, 20

My child, do not forget my teaching, but keep my commands in mind. Trust the LORD with all your heart, and don't depend on your own understanding. Remember the LORD in all you do, and he will give you success. My child, do not reject the LORD's discipline, and don't get angry when he corrects you. The LORD corrects those he loves, just as parents correct the child they delight in.

Proverbs 3:1, 5–6, 11–12

This is what the LORD, who saves you, the Holy One of Israel, says: "I am the LORD your God, who teaches you to do what is good, who leads you in the way you should go."

Isaiah 48:17

The LORD will always lead you. He will satisfy your needs in dry lands and give strength to your bones. You will be like a garden that has much water, like a spring that never runs dry.

Isaiah 58:11

But when the Spirit of truth comes, he will lead

you into all truth. He will not speak his own words, but he will speak only what he hears, and he will tell you what is to come. The Spirit of truth will bring glory to me, because he will take what I have to say and tell it to you.

John 16:13–14

Do not change yourselves to be like the people of this world, but be changed within by a new way of thinking. Then you will be able to decide what God wants for you; you will know what is good and pleasing to him and what is perfect.

Romans 12:2

The true children of God are those who let God's Spirit lead them.

Romans 8:14

Let the peace that Christ gives control your thinking, because you were all called together in one body to have peace. Always be thankful. Let the teaching of Christ live in you richly. Use all wisdom to teach and instruct each other by singing psalms, hymns, and spiritual songs with thankfulness in your hearts to God. Everything you do or say should be done to obey Jesus your Lord. And in all you do, give thanks to God the Father through Jesus.

Colossians 3:15–17

So do not be foolish but learn what the Lord wants you to do.

Ephesians 5:17

TRUTH FROM THE BIBLE ABOUT

Answered Prayer

I will provide for their needs before they ask, and I will help them while they are still asking for help.

Isaiah 65:24

Ask, and God will give to you. Search, and you will find. Knock, and the door will open for you. Yes, everyone who asks will receive. Everyone who searches will find. And everyone who knocks will have the door opened.

Matthew 7:7–8

If you believe, you will get anything you ask for in prayer.

Matthew 21:22

Also, I tell you that if two of you on earth agree about something and pray for it, it will be done for you by my Father in heaven. This is true because if two or three people come together in my name, I am there with them.

Matthew 18:19–20

So I tell you to believe that you have received the things you ask for in prayer, and God will give them to you. When you are praying, if you are angry with someone, forgive him so that your Father in heaven will also forgive your sins.

Mark 11:24–25

And if you ask for anything in my name, I will do it for you so that the Father's glory will be shown through the Son. If you ask me for anything in my name, I will do it.

John 14:13–14

If you remain in me and follow my teachings, you can ask anything you want, and it will be given to you.

John 15:7

When you pray, you should go into your room and close the door and pray to your Father who cannot be seen. Your Father can see what is done in secret, and he will reward you.

Matthew 6:6

In that day you will not ask me for anything. I tell you the truth, my Father will give you anything you ask for in my name.

John 16:23

Let us, then, feel very sure that we can come before God's throne where there is grace. There we can receive mercy and grace to help us when we need it.

Hebrews 4:16

Enjoy serving the LORD, and he will give you what you want. Depend on the LORD; trust him, and he will take care of you.

Psalm 37:4–5

They will call to me, and I will answer them. I will

be with them in trouble; I will rescue them and honor them. I will give them a long, full life, and they will see how I can save.

Psalm 91:15–16

The LORD is close to everyone who prays to him, to all who truly pray to him. He gives those who respect him what they want. He listens when they cry, and he saves them. The LORD protects everyone who loves him, but he will destroy the wicked.

Psalm 145:18–20

The LORD does not listen to the wicked, but he hears the prayers of those who do right.

Proverbs 15:29

These are the words of the LORD, who made the earth, shaped it, and gave it order, whose name is the LORD: "Judah, pray to me, and I will answer you. I will tell you important secrets you have never heard before."

Jeremiah 33:2–3

And God gives us what we ask for because we obey God's commands and do what pleases him. This is what God commands: that we believe in his Son, Jesus Christ, and that we love each other, just as he commanded. The people who obey God's commands live in God, and God lives in them. We know that God lives in us because of the Spirit God gave us.

1 John 3:22–24

Unsaved Loved Ones

They said to him, "Believe in the Lord Jesus and you will be saved—you and all the people in your house."

Acts 16:31

By the words he will say to you, you and all your family will be saved.

Acts 11:14

If a man has a hundred sheep but one of the sheep gets lost, he will leave the other ninety-nine on the hill and go to look for the lost sheep. In the same way, your Father in heaven does not want any of these little children to be lost.

Matthew 18:12, 14

I will pour out water for the thirsty land and make streams flow on dry land. I will pour out my Spirit into your children and my blessing on your descendants. The LORD, the king of Israel, is the LORD All-Powerful, who saves Israel. This is what he says: "I am the beginning and the end. I am the only God."

Isaiah 44:3, 6

The Lord is not slow in doing what he promised—the way some people understand slowness. But God is being patient with you. He does not want anyone to be lost, but he wants all people to change their hearts and lives.

2 Peter 3:9

But test everything. Keep what is good, and stay away from everything that is evil.

1 Thessalonians 5:21–22

Now may God himself, the God of peace, make you pure, belonging only to him. May your whole self—spirit, soul, and body—be kept safe and without fault when our Lord Jesus Christ comes. You can trust the One who calls you to do that for you.

1 Thessalonians 5:23–24

The LORD has made known his power to save; he has shown the other nations his victory for his people. He has remembered his love and his loyalty to the people of Israel. All the ends of the earth have seen God's power to save.

Psalm 98:2–3

Who among you fears the LORD and obeys his servant? That person may walk in the dark and have no light. Then let him trust in the LORD and depend on his God.

Isaiah 50:10

But, God, you will bring down the wicked to the grave. Murderers and liars will live only half a lifetime. But I will trust in you.

Psalm 55:23

This is what the LORD says: "Give justice to all people, and do what is right, because my salvation will come to you soon. Soon everyone will know that I do what is right."

Isaiah 56:1

But I tell you the truth, it is better for you that I go away. When I go away, I will send the Helper to you. If I do not go away, the Helper will not come. When the Helper comes, he will prove to the people of the world the truth about sin, about being right with God, and about judgment. He will prove to them that sin is not believing in me.

John 16:7–9

Train children how to live right, and when they are old, they will not change.

Proverbs 22:6

TRUTH FROM THE BIBLE ABOUT

Your Family

But if you don't want to serve the LORD, you must choose for yourselves today whom you will serve. You may serve the gods that your ancestors worshiped when they lived on the other side of the Euphrates River, or you may serve the gods of the Amorites who lived in this land. As for me and my family, we will serve the LORD.

Joshua 24:15

When you talk, do not say harmful things, but say what people need—words that will help others become stronger. Then what you say will do good to those who listen to you. And do not make the Holy Spirit sad. The Spirit is God's proof that you belong to him. God gave you the Spirit to show that God will make you free when the final day comes. Do not be bitter or angry or mad. Never shout angrily or say things to hurt others. Never do anything evil. Be kind and loving to each other, and forgive each other just as God forgave you in Christ.

Ephesians 4:29–32

Train children how to live right, and when they are old, they will not change.

Proverbs 22:6

They said to him, "Believe in the Lord Jesus and you will be saved—you and all the people in your house."

Acts 16:31

Honor your father and your mother so that you will live a long time in the land that the LORD your God is going to give you.

Exodus 20:12

What I say is true: Anyone wanting to become an elder desires a good work. He must be a good family leader, having children who cooperate with full respect. (If someone does not know how to lead the family, how can that person take care of God's church?)

1 Timothy 3:1, 4–5

Children are a gift from the LORD; babies are a reward. Children who are born to a young man are like arrows in the hand of a warrior. Happy is the man who has his bag full of arrows. They will not be defeated when they fight their enemies at the city gate.

Psalm 127:3–5

Elijah will help parents love their children and children love their parents. Otherwise, I will come and put a curse on the land.

Malachi 4:6

Old people are proud of their grandchildren, and children are proud of their parents. A friend loves you all the time, and a brother helps in time of trouble. A foolish son makes his father sad and causes his mother great sorrow.

Proverbs 17:6, 17, 25

Always remember these commands I give you today. Teach them to your children, and talk about them when you sit at home and walk along the road, when you lie down and when you get up. Write them down and tie them to your hands as a sign. Tie them on your forehead to remind you, and write them on your doors and gates.

Deuteronomy 6:6–9

Correct your children, and you will be proud; they will give you satisfaction. Where there is no word from God, people are uncontrolled, but those who obey what they have been taught are happy.

Proverbs 29:17–18

Good people leave their wealth to their grandchildren, but a sinner's wealth is stored up for good people.

Proverbs 13:22

Happy are those who respect the Lord and obey him. You will enjoy what you work for, and you will be blessed with good things.

Psalm 128:1–2

The father of a good child is very happy; parents who have wise children are glad because of them. Make your father and mother happy; give your mother a reason to be glad.

Proverbs 23:24–25

My child, listen and accept what I say. Then you will have a long life. I am guiding you in the way of wisdom, and I am leading you on the right path.

Proverbs 4:10–11

Now, brothers and sisters, we ask you to appreciate those who work hard among you, who lead you in the Lord and teach you. Respect them with a very special love because of the work they do. Live in peace with each other. We ask you, brothers and sisters, to warn those who do not work. Encourage the people who are afraid. Help those who are weak. Be patient with everyone. Be sure that no one pays back wrong for wrong, but always try to do what is good for each other and for all people.

1 Thessalonians 5:12–15

God has chosen you and made you his holy people. He loves you. So always do these things: Show mercy to others, be kind, humble, gentle, and patient. Get along with each other, and forgive each other. If someone does wrong to you, forgive that person because the Lord forgave you.

Colossians 3:12–13

But the Spirit produces the fruit of love, joy peace, patience, kindness, goodness, faithfulness, gentleness, self-control. There is no law that says these things are wrong. Those who belong to Christ Jesus have crucified their own sinful selves. They have given up their old selfish feelings and the evil things they wanted to do.

Galatians 5:22–24

Let the peace that Christ gives control your thinking, because you were all called together in one body to have peace. Always be thankful. Let the teaching of Christ live in you richly. Use all wisdom to teach and instruct each other by singing psalms, hymns, and spiritual songs with thankfulness in your hearts to God. Everything you do or say should be done to obey Jesus your Lord. And in all you do, give thanks to God the Father through Jesus.

Colossians 3:15–17

I give you a new command; Love each other. You must love each other as I have loved you. All people will know that you are my followers if you love each other.

John 13:34–35

Always be humble, gentle, and patient, accepting each other in love. You are joined together with peace through the Spirit, so make every effort to continue together in this way.

Ephesians 4:2–3

Yield to obey each other because you respect Christ.

Ephesians 5:21

Do everything without complaining or arguing. Then you will be innocent and without any wrong. You will be

God's children without fault. But you are living with crooked and mean people all around you, among whom you shine like stars in the dark world.

Philippians 2:14–15

My son, pay attention to my wisdom; listen to my words of understanding. Be careful to use good sense, and watch what you say.

Proverbs 5:1–2

Children, obey your parents as the Lord wants, because this is the right thing to do. The command says, "Honor your father and mother." This is the first command that has a promise with it—"Then everything will be well with you, and you will have a long life on the earth."

Ephesians 6:1–3

Love each other like brothers and sisters. Give each other more honor than you want for yourselves. Do not be lazy but work hard, serving the Lord with all your heart. Be joyful because you have hope. Be patient when trouble comes, and pray at all times. Share with God's people who need help. Bring strangers in need into your homes.

Romans 12:10–13

Being respected is more important than having great riches. To be well thought of is better than silver or gold.

Proverbs 22:1

Singles

And I will make you my promised bride forever. I will be good and fair; I will show you my love and mercy.

Hosea 2:19

Now for those who are not married and for the widows I say this: It is good for them to stay unmarried as I am. But if they cannot control themselves, they should marry. It is better to marry than to burn with sexual desire. But in any case each one of you should continue to live the way God has given you to live— the way you were when God called you. This is a rule I make in all the churches.

1 Corinthians 7:8–9, 17

But if you decide to marry, you have not sinned. And if a girl who has never married decides to marry, she has not sinned. But those who marry will have trouble in this life, and I want you to be free from trouble.

1 Corinthians 7:28

I want you to be free from worry. A man who is not married is busy with the Lord's work, trying to please the Lord. But a man who is married is busy with things of the world, trying to please his wife. I am saying this to help you, not to limit you. But I

want you to live in the right way, to give yourselves
fully to the Lord without concern for other things.

1 Corinthians 7:32–33, 35

Marriage should be honored by everyone, and
husband and wife should keep their marriage pure.
God will judge as guilty those who take part in sexual
sins.

Hebrews 13:4

Because you have these blessings, do your best to
add these things to your lives: to your faith, add goodness; and to your goodness, add knowledge; and to your
knowledge, add self-control; and to your self-control,
add patience; and to your patience, add service for God;
and to your service for God, add kindness for your
brothers and sisters in Christ; and to this kindness,
add love. If all these things are in you and are growing,
they will help you to be useful and productive in your
knowledge of our Lord Jesus Christ.

2 Peter 1:5–8

If a man thinks he is not doing the right thing with
the girl he is engaged to, if she is almost past the best age
to marry and he feels he should marry her, he should
do what he wants. They should get married. It is no sin.
But if a man is sure in his mind that there is no need for
marriage, and has his own desires under control, and has
decided not to marry the one to whom he is engaged, he
is doing the right thing.

1 Corinthians 7:36–37

Trust the LORD with all your heart, and don't depend on your own understanding. Remember the LORD in all you do, and he will give you success. Don't depend on your own wisdom. Respect the LORD and refuse to do wrong.

Proverbs 3:5–7

Enjoy serving the LORD, and he will give you what you want.

Psalm 37:4

In the same way, my brothers and sisters, your old selves died, and you became free from the law through the body of Christ. This happened so that you might belong to someone else—the One who was raised from the dead—and so that we might be used in service to God.

Romans 7:4

Each person should judge his own actions and not compare himself with others. Then he can be proud for what he himself has done.

Galatians 6:4

Marriage

The LORD God used the rib from the man to make a woman, and then he brought the woman to the man.

Genesis 2:22

When a man finds a wife, he finds something good. It shows that the LORD is pleased with him.

Proverbs 18:22

Get married and have sons and daughters. Find wives for your sons, and let your daughters be married so they also may have sons and daughters.

Jeremiah 29:6

And I will make you my promised bride forever. I will be good and fair; I will show you my love and mercy. I will be true to you as my promised bride, and you will know the LORD.

Hosea 2:19–20

But because sexual sin is a danger, each man should have his own wife, and each woman should have her own husband. The husband should give his wife all that he owes her as his wife. And the wife should give her husband all that she owes him as her husband. The wife does not have full rights over her own body; her husband shares them. And the husband does not have full rights over his own body; his wife shares them. Do not refuse to give your bodies to each other, unless you both agree to stay away from sexual relations for a time so you can give your time to prayer. Then come together again so Satan cannot tempt you because of a lack of self-control.

1 Corinthians 7:2–5

So I want the younger widows to marry, have children, and manage their homes. Then no enemy will have any reason to criticize them.

1 Timothy 5:14

In the same way, you wives should yield to your husbands. Then, if some husbands do not obey God's teaching, they will be persuaded to believe without anyone's saying a word to them. They will be persuaded by the way their wives live. Your husbands will see the pure lives you live with your respect for God.

1 Peter 3:1–2

So God created human beings in his image. In the image of God he created them. He created them male and female. God blessed them and said, "Have many children and grow in number. Fill the earth and be its master. Rule over the fish in the sea and over the birds in the sky and over every living thing that moves on the earth."

Genesis 1:27–28

Marriage should be honored by everyone, and husband and wife should keep their marriage pure. God will judge as guilty those who take part in sexual sins.

Hebrews 13:4

Yield to obey each other because you respect Christ. Wives, yield to your husbands, as you do to the Lord, because the husband is the head of the wife, as Christ is the head of the church. And he is the Savior of the body, which is the church. Husbands, love your wives as Christ loved the church and gave himself for it to make it belong to God. Christ used the word to make the church clean by washing it with water. He died so that he could give the church to himself like a bride in all her beauty. He died so that the church could be pure and without fault, with no evil or sin or any other wrong thing in it. In the same way, husbands should love their wives as they love their own bodies. The man who loves his wife loves himself. No one ever hates his own body, but feeds and takes care of it. And that is what Christ does for the church, because we are parts of his body. The Scripture says, "So a man will leave his father and mother and be united with his wife, and the two will become one body." That secret is very important—I am talking about Christ and the church. But each one of you must love his wife as he loves himself, and a wife must respect her husband.

Ephesians 5:21–23, 25–33

In the same say, you husbands should live with your wives in an understanding way, since they are weaker than you. But show them respect, because God gives them the same blessing he gives you—the grace that gives true life. Do this so that nothing will stop your prayers.

1 Peter 3:7

You are not the same as those who do not believe. So do not join yourselves to them. Good and bad do not belong together. Light and darkness cannot share together. How can Christ and Belial, the devil, have any agreement? What can a believer have together with a nonbeliever? The temple of God cannot have any agreement with idols, and we are the temple of the living God. As God said: "I will live with them and walk with them. And I will be their God, and they will be my people."

2 Corinthians 6:14–16

If you love me, you will obey my commands.

John 14:15

Jesus answered, "Love the Lord your God with all your heart, all your soul, and all your mind. This is the first and most important command. And the second command is like the first: Love your neighbor as you love yourself."

Matthew 22:37–39

Let us think about each other and help each other to show love and do good deeds.

Hebrews 10:24

What You Can Do
to . . .

WHAT YOU CAN DO TO

Make Better Use of Your Time

Teach us how short our lives really are so that we may be wise.

Psalm 90:12

Jesus said to them, "The Father is the only One who has the authority to decide dates and times. These things are not for you to know."

Acts 1:7

Do people really gain anything from their work? I saw the hard work God has given people to do. God has given them a desire to know the future. He does everything just right and on time, but people can never completely understand what he is doing. So I realize that the best thing for them is to be happy and enjoy themselves as long as they live. God wants all people to eat and drink and be happy in their work, which are gifts from God. I know that everything God does will continue forever. People cannot add anything to what God has done, and they cannot take anything away from it. God does it this way to make people respect him.

Ecclesiastes 3:9–14

Whoever obeys the king's command will be safe. A wise person does the right thing at the right time. There is a right time and a right way for everything, yet people often have many troubles. They do not know what the future holds, and no one can tell them what will happen.

Ecclesiastes 8:5–7

Don't wear yourself out trying to get rich; be wise enough to control yourself. Wealth can vanish in the wink of an eye. It can seem to grow wings and fly away like an eagle.

Proverbs 23:4–5

Anyone who loves learning accepts correction, but a person who hates being corrected is stupid.

Proverbs 12:1

Spend time with the wise and you will become wise, but the friends of fools will suffer.

Proverbs 13:20

A friend loves you all the time, and a brother helps in time of trouble.

Proverbs 17:17

A lazy person will end up poor, but a hard worker will become rich. Those who gather crops on time are wise, but those who sleep through the harvest are a disgrace.

Proverbs 10:4–5

Hard workers will become leaders, but those who are lazy will be slaves.

Proverbs 12:24

If someone is lazy, the roof will begin to fall. If he doesn't fix it, the house will leak.

Ecclesiastes 10:18

The right word spoken at the right time is as beautiful as gold apples in a silver bowl.

Proverbs 25:11

My child, pay attention to my words; listen closely to what I say. Don't ever forget my words; keep them always in mind. They are the key to life for those who find them; they bring health to the whole body. Be careful what you think, because your thoughts run your life. Don't use your mouth to tell lies; don't ever say things that are not true. Keep your eyes focused on what is right, and look straight ahead to what is good. Be careful what you do, and always do what is right.

Proverbs 4:20–26

The LORD sees everything you do, and he watches where you go.

Proverbs 5:21

Please God

Bring to me all the people who are mine, whom I made for my glory, whom I formed and made. The people I made will sing songs to praise me.

Isaiah 43:7, 21

The time is coming when the true worshipers will worship the Father in spirit and truth, and that time is here already. You see, the Father too is actively seeking such people to worship him. God is spirit, and those who worship him must worship in spirit and truth.

John 4:23–24

Those who blew the trumpets and those who sang together sounded like one person as they praised and thanked the LORD. They sang as others played their trumpets, cymbals, and other instruments. They praised the Lord with this sing: "He is good; his love continues forever." Then the Temple of the LORD was filled with a cloud. The priests could not continue their work because of the cloud, because the LORD's glory filled the Temple of God.

2 Chronicles 5:13–14

You also are like living stones, so let yourselves be used to build a spiritual temple—to be holy priests who offer spiritual sacrifices to God. He will accept those sacrifices through Jesus Christ. But you are a chosen people, royal priests, a holy nation, a people for God's own possession. You were chosen to tell about the wonderful acts of God, who called you out of darkness into his wonderful light.

1 Peter 2:5, 9

So through Jesus let us always offer to God our sacrifice of praise, coming from lips that speak his name. Do not forget to do good to others, and share with them, because such sacrifices please God.

Hebrews 13:15–16

You are worthy, our Lord and God, to receive glory and honor and power, because you made all things. Everything existed and was made, because you wanted it.

Revelation 4:11

Without faith no one can please God. Anyone who comes to God must believe that he is real and that he rewards those who truly want to find him.

Hebrews 11:6

We pray that you will also have great wisdom and understanding in spiritual things so that you will live the kind of life that honors and pleases the Lord in every way. You will produce fruit in every good work and grow in the knowledge of God.

Colossians 1:9b–10

So brothers and sisters, since God has shown us great mercy, I beg you to offer your lives as a living sacrifice to him. Your offering must be only for God and pleasing to him, which is the spiritual way for you to worship. Do not change yourselves to be like the people of this world, but be changed within by a new way of thinking. Then you will be able to decide what God wants for you; you will know what is good and pleasing to him and what is perfect.

Romans 12:1–2

First, I tell you to pray for all people, asking God for what they need and being thankful to him. This is good, and it pleases God our Savior. So, I want the men everywhere to pray, lifting up their hands in a holy manner, without anger and arguments.

1 Timothy 2:1, 3, 8

I will praise the LORD. Let everyone praise his holy name forever.

Psalm 145:21

I will thank the LORD very much; I will praise him in front of my people.

Psalm 109:30

Clap your hands, all you people. Shout to God with joy.

Psalm 47:1

The LORD is pleased with those who respect him, with those who trust his love.

Psalm 147:11

Praise the LORD! Sing a new song to the LORD; sing his praise in the meeting of his people. Let the

Israelites be happy because of God, their Maker. Let the people of Jerusalem rejoice because of their King. They should praise him with dancing. They should sing praises to him with tambourines and harps. The LORD is pleased with his people; he saves the humble. Let those who worship him rejoice in his glory. Let them sing for joy even in bed! Let them shout his praise.

Psalm 149:1–6a

Those people who are ruled by their sinful selves cannot please God. But you are not ruled by your sinful selves. You are ruled by the Spirit, if that Spirit of God really lives in you.

Romans 8:8–9a

And God gives us what we ask for because we obey God's commands and do what pleases him.

1 John 3:22

It is not fancy hair, gold jewelry, or fine clothes that should make you beautiful. No, your beauty should come from within you—the beauty of a gentle and quiet spirit that will never be destroyed and is very precious to God.

1 Peter 3:3–4

But the LORD said to Samuel, "Don't look at how handsome Eliab is or how tall he is, because I have not chosen him. God does not see the same way people see. People look at the outside of a person, but the LORD looks at the heart."

1 Samuel 16:7

Since we know what it means to fear the LORD, we try to help people accept the truth about us. God knows what we really are, and I hope that in your hearts you know, too. We are not trying to prove ourselves to you again, but we are telling you about ourselves so you will be proud of us. Then you will have an answer for those who are proud about things that can be seen rather than what is in the heart.

2 Corinthians 5:11–12

But if we confess our sins, he will forgive our sins, because we can trust God to do what is right. He will cleanse us from all the wrongs we have done.

1 John 1:9

Grow in the Spirit

But grow in the grace and knowledge of our LORD and Savior Jesus Christ. Glory be to him now and forever! Amen.

2 Peter 3:18

As newborn babies want milk, you should want the pure and simple teaching. By it you can grow up and be saved, because you have already examined and seen how good the Lord is.

1 Peter 2:2–3

Make every effort to give yourself to God as the kind of person he will accept. Be a worker who is not ashamed and who uses the true teaching in the right way.

2 Timothy 2:15

Continue to do those things; give your life to doing them so your progress may be seen by everyone.

1 Timothy 4:15

So let us go on to grown-up teaching. Let us not go back over the beginning lessons we learned about Christ. We should not again start teaching about faith in God and about turning away from those acts that lead to death.

Hebrews 6:1

Because you have these blessings, do your best to add these things to your lives: to your faith, add goodness; and to your goodness, add knowledge; and to your knowledge, add self-control; and to your self-control, add patience; and to your patience, add service for God; and to your service for God, add kindness for your brothers and sisters in Christ; and to this kindness, add love. If all these things are in you and are growing, they will help you to be useful and productive in your knowledge of our Lord Jesus Christ.

2 Peter 1:5–8

So I bow in prayer before the Father from whom every family in heaven and on earth gets its true name. I ask the Father in his great glory to give you the power to be strong inwardly through his Spirit. I pray that Christ will live in your hearts by faith and that your life will be strong in love and be built on love. And I pray that you and all God's holy people will have the power to understand the greatness of Christ's love—how wide and how long and how high and how deep that love is. Christ's love is greater than anyone can ever know, but I pray that you will be able to know that love. Then you can be filled with the fullness of God.

Ephesians 3:14–19

Because of this, since the day we heard about you, we have continued praying for you, asking God that you will know fully what he wants. We pray that you will also have great wisdom and understanding in spiritual things so that you will live the kind of live that honors and pleases the Lord in every way. You will produce fruit in every good work and grow in the knowledge of God. God will strengthen you with his own great power so that you will not give up when troubles come, but you will be patient.

Colossians 1:9–11

Let the teaching of Christ live in you richly. Use all wisdom to teach and instruct each other by singing psalms, hymns, and spiritual songs with thankfulness in your hearts to God.

Colossians 3:16

Our faces, then, are not covered. We all show the Lord's glory, and we are being changed to be like him. This change in us brings ever greater glory, which comes from the Lord, who is the Spirit.

2 Corinthians 3:18

Like trees planted in the Temple of the Lord, they will grow strong in the courtyards of our God.

Psalm 92:13

God began doing a good work in you, and I am sure he will continue it until it is finished when Jesus Christ comes again. This is my prayer for you: that your love will grow more and more; that you will have knowledge and understanding with your love; that you will see the difference between good and bad and will choose the good; that you will be pure and without wrong for the coming of Christ.

Philippians 1:6, 9–10

Then we will no longer be babies. We will not be tossed about like a ship that the waves carry one way and then another. We will not be influenced by every new teaching we hear from people who are trying to fool us. They make plans and try any kind of trick to fool people into following the wrong path. No! Speaking the truth with love, we will grow up in every way into Christ, who is the head. The whole body depends on Christ, and all the parts of the body are joined and held together. Each part does its own work to make the whole body grow and be strong with love.

Ephesians 4:14–16

WHAT YOU CAN DO TO

Influence Your World

You are the light that gives light to the world. A city that is built on a hill cannot be hidden. And people don't hide a light under a bowl. They put it on the lampstand so the light shines for all the people in the house. In the same way, you should be a light for other people. Live so that they will see the good things you do and will praise your Father in heaven.

Matthew 5:14–16

The wise people will shine like the brightness of the sky. Those who teach others to live right will shine like stars forever and ever.

Daniel 12:3

Jesus said to his followers, "Go everywhere in the world and tell the Good News to every one. Anyone who believes and is baptized will be saved, but anyone who does not believe will be punished. And those who believe will be able to do these things as proof: They will use my name to force out demons. They will speak in new languages. They will pick up snakes and drink poison without being hurt. They will touch the sick, and the sick will be healed." After the Lord Jesus said these things to his followers, he was carried up into heaven, and he sat at the right side of God. The followers went everywhere in the world and told the Good News to people, and the Lord helped them. The Lord proved that the Good News they told was true by giving them power to work miracles.

Mark 16:15–20

But when the Holy Spirit comes to you, you will receive power. You will be my witnesses—in Jerusalem, in all of Judea, in Samaria, and in every part of the world.

Acts 1:8

The Lord has put his Spirit in me, because he appointed me to tell the Good News to the poor. He has sent me to tell the captives they are free and to tell the blind that they can see again. God sent me to free those who have been treated unfairly and to announce the time when the Lord will show his kindness.

Luke 4:18

I tell you the truth, whoever believes in me will do the same things that I do. Those who believe will do even greater things than these, because I am going to the Father.

John 14:12

I give you a new command: Love each other. You must love each other as I have loved you. All people will know that you are my followers if you love each other.

John 13:34–35

Jacob's well was there. Jesus was tired from his long trip, so he sat down beside the well. It was about twelve o'clock noon. Jesus told her, "Go get your husband and come back here." The woman answered, "I have no husband." Then the woman left her water jar and went back to town. She said to the people, "Come and see a man who told me everything I ever did. Do you think he might be the Christ?" So the people left the town and went to see Jesus.

John 4:6, 16–17, 28–30

Loving God means obeying his commands. And God's commands are not too hard for us, because everyone who is a child of God conquers the world. And this is the victory that conquers the world—our faith. So the one who wins against the world is the person who believes that Jesus is the Son of God.

1 John 5:3–5

Faith means being sure of the things we hope for and knowing that something is real even if we do not see it. Faith is the reason we remember great people who lived in the past. It is by faith we understand that the whold world was made by God's command so what we see was made by something that cannot be seen. Do I need to give more examples? I do not have time to tell you about Gideon, Barak, Samson, Jephthah, David, Samuel, and the prophets. Through their faith they defeated kingdoms. They did what was right, received God's promises, and shut the mouths of lions. They stopped great fires and were saved from being killed with swords. They were weak, and yet were made strong. They were powerful in battle and defeated other armies.

Hebrews 11:1–3, 32–34

God loved the world so much that he gave his one and only Son so that whoever believes in him may not be lost, but have eternal life.

John 3:16

But the Spirit produces the fruit of love, joy, peace, patience, kindness, goodness, faithfulness, gentleness, self-control. There is no law that says these things are wrong.

Galatians 5:22–23

The whole law is made complete in this one command: "Love your neighbor as you love yourself."

Galatians 5:14

Do not change yourselves to be like the people of this world, but be changed within by a new way of thinking. Then you will be able to decide what God wants for you; you will know what is good and pleasing to him and what is perfect.

Romans 12:2

In all the work you are doing, work the best you can. Work as if you were doing it for the Lord, not for people. Remember that you will receive your reward from the Lord, which he promised to his people. You are serving the Lord Christ.

Colossians 3:23–24

But you are a chosen people, royal priests, a holy nation, a people for God's own possession. You were chosen to tell about the wonderful acts of God, who called you out of darkness into his wonderful light. At one time you were not a people, but now you are God's people. In the past you have never received mercy, but now you have received God's mercy. Dear friends, you are like foreigners and strangers in this world. I beg you to avoid the evil things your bodies want to do that fight against your soul. People who do not believe are living all around you and might say that you are doing wrong. Live such good lives that they will see the good things you do and will give glory to God on the day when Christ comes again.

1 Peter 2:9–12

In the past, people did not understand God, and he ignored this. But now, God tells all people in the world to change their hearts and lives.

Acts 17:30

But before people can ask the Lord for help, they must believe in him; and before they can believe in him, they must hear about him; and for them to hear about the Lord, someone must tell them.

Romans 10:14

This is my command: Love each other as I have loved you. The greatest love a person can show is to die for his friends.

John 15:12–13

The Father is the One who sent me. No one can come to me unless the Father draws him to me, and I will raise that person up on the last day.

John 6:44

After they had prayed, the place where they were meeting was shaken. They were all filled with the Holy Spirit, and they spoke God's word without fear.

Acts 4:31

Jesus answered, "Everyone who drinks this water will be thirsty again, but whoever drinks the water I give will never be thirsty. The water I give will become a spring of water gushing up inside that person, giving eternal life."

John 4:13–14

Count Your Blessings

You are descendants of the prophets. You have received the agreement God made with your ancestors. He said to your father Abraham, "Through your descendants all the nations on the earth will be blessed."

Acts 3:25

As the Scripture says, "Anyone who trusts in him will never be disappointed." That Scripture says "anyone" because there is no difference between those who are Jews and those who are not. The same Lord is the Lord of all and gives many blessings to all who trust in him, as the Scripture says, "Anyone who calls on the Lord will be saved."

Romans 10:11–13

The believers in Macedonia and Southern Greece were happy to give their money to help the poor among God's people at Jerusalem. They were happy to do this, and really they owe it to them. These who are not Jews have shared in the Jews' spiritual blessings, so they should use their material possessions to help the Jews.

Romans 15:26–27

Some people are like land that gets plenty of rain. The land produces a good crop for those who work it, and it receives God's blessings. Other people are like land that grows thorns and weeds and is worthless. It is in danger of being cursed by God and will be destroyed by fire.

Hebrews 6:7–8

Some people brought their little children to Jesus so he could touch them, but his followers told them to stop. When Jesus saw this, he was upset and said to them, "Let the little children come to me. Don't stop them, because the kingdom of God belongs to people who are like these children. I tell you the truth, you must accept the kingdom of God as if you were a little child, or you will never enter it." Then Jesus took the children in his arms, put his hands on them, and blessed them.

Mark 10:13–16

Because he was full of grace and truth, from him we all received one gift after another. The law was given through Moses, but grace and truth came through Jesus Christ.

John 1:16–17

Give thanks to the LORD because he is good. His love continues forever.

Psalm 136:1

Every good action and every perfect gift is from God. These good gifts come down from the Creator of the sun, moon, and stars, who does not change like their shifting shadows. God decided to give us life through the word of truth so we might be the most important of all the things he made.

James 1:17–18

Praise be to the God and Father of our Lord Jesus Christ. In Christ, God has given us every spiritual blessing in the heavenly world. That is, in Christ, he chose us before the world was made so that we would be his holy people—people without blame before him.

Ephesians 1:3–4

Most importantly, love each other deeply, because love will cause many sins to be forgiven.

1 Peter 4:8

Riches and honor come from you. You rule everything. You have the power and strength to make anyone great and strong. Now, our God, we thank you and praise your glorious name.

1 Chronicles 29:12–13

When you have all you want to eat, then praise the Lord your God for giving you a good land.

Deuteronomy 8:10

Thanks be to God for his gift that is too wonderful for words.

2 Corinthians 9:15

Open for me the Temple gates. Then I will come in and thank the Lord. This is the Lord's gate; only those who are good may enter through it.

Lord, I thank you for answering me. You have saved me.

Psalm 118:19–21

The people crossed the Jordan on the tenth day of the first month and camped at Gilgal, east of Jericho. They carried with them the twelve rocks taken from the Jordan, and Joshua set them up at Gilgal. Then he spoke to the Israelites: "In the future your children will ask you, 'What do these rocks mean.' Tell them, 'Israel crossed the Jordan River on dry land. The Lord your God caused the water to stop flowing until you finished crossing it, just as the Lord did to the Red Sea. He stopped the water until we crossed it. The Lord did this so all people would know he has great power and so you would always respect the Lord your God."

Joshua 4:19–24

We always thank God for all of you and mention you when we pray. We continually recall before God our Father the things you have done because of your faith and the work you have done because of your love. And we thank him that you continue to be strong because of your hope in our Lord Jesus Christ.

1 Thessalonians 1:2–3

Always give thanks to God the Father for everything, in the name of our Lord Jesus Christ.

Ephesians 5:20

God's Plan of Salvation

Sin came into the world because of what one man did, and with sin came death. This is why everyone must die—because everyone sinned.

Romans 5:12

All have sinned and are not good enough for God's glory, and all need to be made right with God by his grace, which is a free gift. They need to be made free from sin through Jesus Christ.

Romans 3:23–24

When people sin, they earn what sin pays—death. But God gives us a free gift—life forever in Christ Jesus our Lord.

Romans 6:23

But God shows his great love for us in this way: Christ died for us while we were still sinners.

Romans 5:8

Now, brothers and sisters, I want you to remember the Good News I brought to you. You received this Good News and continue strong in it. And you are being saved by it if you continue believing what I told you. If you do not, then you believed for nothing. I passed on to you what I received, of which this was most important: that Christ died for our sins, as the Scriptures say; that he was buried and was raised to life on the third day as the Scriptures say.

1 Corinthians 15:1–4

God did not send his Son into the world to judge the world guilty, but to save the world through him.

John 3:17

Those who believe in the Son have eternal life, but those who do not obey the Son will never have life. God's anger stays on them.

John 3:36

God loved the world so much that he gave his one and only Son so that whoever believes in him may not be lost, but have eternal life.

John 3:16

But to all who did accept him and believe in him he gave the right to become children of God.

John 1:12

I mean that you have been saved by grace through believing. You did not save yourselves; it was a gift from God. It was not the result of your own efforts, so you cannot brag about it.

Ephesians 2:8–9

Here I am! I stand at the door and knock. If you hear my voice and open the door, I will come in and eat with you, and you will eat with me.

Revelation 3:20

This is what the Scripture says: "The word is near you; it is in your mouth and in your heart." That is the teaching of faith that we are telling. If you use your mouth to say, "Jesus is Lord," and if you believe in your heart that God raised Jesus from the dead, you will be saved. We believe with our hearts, and so we are made right with God. And we use our mouths to say that we believe, and so we are saved.

Romans 10:8–10

All those who stand before others and say they believe in me, I will say before my Father in heaven that they belong to me.

Matthew 10:32

This is what God told us: God has given us eternal life, and this life is in his Son. Whoever has the Son has life, but whoever does not have the Son of God does not have life. I write this letter to you who believe in the Son of God so you will know you have eternal life.

1 John 5:11–13

Notes

Notes

Notes

Notes

Notes

Notes

Notes

Notes

Notes